MURDER IN THE CATHEDRAL

MURDER
IN THE CATHEDRAL

by

T. S. ELIOT

With an introduction and notes

by

NEVILL COGHILL

An Educational Edition

ff

faber and faber

LONDON · BOSTON

First published in June 1935
First published in this Educational Edition 1965
by Faber and Faber Limited
3 Queen Square London WC1
Reprinted 1965 (twice), 1967 (twice), 1968,
1975, 1981, 1983 and 1985
Printed in Great Britain by
Richard Clay (The Chaucer Press) Ltd,
Bungay, Suffolk
All rights reserved

ISBN 0 571 06327 6 (educational paper)

© 1965 Introduction and Notes
by Nevill Coghill

CONTENTS

INTRODUCTION

Mr. Eliot accepted the commission to write a play for the
Canterbury Festival of June 1935, at the request of George
Bell, Bishop of Chichester, and he chose for his subject-
matter the martyrdom of the most famous of all English
Saints, Thomas Becket, who was Archbishop of Canterbury
between the years 1162 and 1170, when he was brutally
murdered, on the twenty-ninth of December, in his own
cathedral church. The assassins[1] were four knights,
Reginald Fitz Urse, William de Traci, Hugh de Morville
and Richard Brito. When they had accomplished what they
had come to do if Becket proved stubborn, they left the
precincts shouting that they were the King's men; and indeed in fairness to their bloody-minded and reckless feu-
dality it must be said they probably believed themselves to
be acting in consonance with a half-expressed wish of his in
the matter, in a long-drawn-out but not entirely straight
fight between Crown and Church on certain constitutional
issues. To them Becket appeared an arrogant and turbulent
priest, a traitor whittling away the rightful and reasonable
powers of their supreme overlord, Henry II, and his suc-
cessors; to Becket and his fellow-monks it was a spiritual
conflict, an incident in the eternal struggle of Good and
Evil in which they happened to be all-importantly involved; to the monks, and, later, to the Christian world,
Becket was God's champion, *agonotheta Dei*,[2] *athleta
Christi*;[3] it had the air of a naked war between Black and
White, each side believing itself to be the latter.

The story is richly documented, but all the documents

issue from the supporters of Becket; there exist at least eleven eye-witness accounts, written down immediately after the event, by monks of Canterbury for the most part, and these are the sources on which Eliot drew for the facts of the case.

He has treated their evidence faithfully but selectively, to give the form and concentration of art to the natural hubbub of murder; almost everything in his dialogue has its basis in one or other account so that what he has written is imagined, not invented. At the same time many an incident, and in particular one of the most touching—an elderly monk, Edward Grim, raised his arm to protect the Archbishop's head from the first sword-thrust of Reginald Fitz Urse, and it was sliced through[4]—is left out as not germane to the true theme of the play; for this is not a Shakespearean chronicle-play that tells an intricate, proliferating story full of incident, but a sparer drama, more in the manner of Aeschylus, about a great cause in which incident and idiosyncrasy lose their importance. Unlike Shakespeare's plays, all of which take and give delight in the excitements of narrative, Eliot's plays are about situations, not stories, like *Everyman* before them, and *Waiting for Godot* after. *Murder in the Cathedral* is about a situation and a quality of life; the situation is perpetual and the quality is rare.

It is the first crest of Eliot's dramatic achievement and it is interesting to stand on the crest and look back over the paths by which he seems to have reached it and see the pattern of a growing design furthered by accident, a design that begins in a sad, liberal agnosticism and steadily strengthens into the positive grief-in-joy and joy-in-grief of Christianity, that includes what we call tragedy and goes beyond it. The pattern spreads over many years, some twenty at least, to put it in round numbers, and the first threads of it are perceptible in Eliot's earliest published poetry. It can be traced from *The Love Song of J. Alfred Prufrock* (1917) and *The Waste Land* (1922) both of which pose a problem in the purpose of life and begin faintly to formulate a solution, and these reappear with many variations of form and manner in the works that followed, *The Hollow Men* (1925), *Ash Wednesday* (1930) and, most strangely, in *Sweeney Agonistes* (1926/7). At last they took fully Christian shape in *The Rock* (1934), which has the air of a trial run for *Murder in the Cathedral*, when their essentials are compared.

It is of course no accident that the change from agnosticism to Christianity should gradually have emerged in Eliot's writing, since it took place in his life, and was marked by the publication of a book of essays that proclaimed it, *For Lancelot Andrewes* (1928). The progress of his thought, both in poetry and prose, wears the look of an intention discovering itself; but accident is woven into the pattern too, for the occasion that called forth *The Rock* was not of Eliot's seeking, any more than the occasion of *Murder in the Cathedral*. I will try to indicate this pattern of progress in so far as it breaks surface in his earlier works.

The Love Song of J. Alfred Prufrock is the sad soliloquy of one no longer in his first youth, feeling his path through a London fog, on his way to visit a lady whom, it would seem, he loves. He is oppressed by a problem he would like to lay before her, and yet more oppressed by the fear that she may dismiss both it and him as tiresomely irrelevant. She is evidently a cultivated intellectual, moving easily among the sophisticated women who 'come and go, talking of Michelangelo'; but will she understand 'the overwhelming question' he longs to ask, but which in fact he never gets so far as even to formulate? He is shy of mentioning it to the reader whom he has invited to accompany him; for who is he to disturb the universe with questions? Yet his question, though never asked, is indicated. It is a question that only Lazarus, come back from the dead, can answer; or so he suggests. It is therefore some question that calls for an answer from beyond death and time and space, from some enfolding but unknowable world of supernatural life, which cannot be acknowledged, or even talked about, by virtuous agnostics. But if Prufrock does not dare to ask it, the significance of the poem is that he feels the oppressive need to do so, or to move out into a region where such questions are possible.

In *The Waste Land* the poet's desolation is not caused by a sense of fog-bound intellectualist voices in which he feels himself drowning, but by the deeper desolation of a world declining into materialism. His great question is harder than before to ask; yet a kind of answer from some further region is faintly hinted:

> Who is the third who walks always beside you?
> When I count, there are only you and I together
> But when I look ahead up the white road
> There is always another one walking beside you
> Gliding wrapt in a brown mantle, hooded
> I do not know whether a man or a woman
> —But who is that on the other side of you?

Eliot's note on this passage refers us to an Antarctic expedition, on which an unknown presence was felt at the side of the explorers, trudging through a dangerous waste of snow; but the lines are also intended to recall by their mention of 'a brown mantle', the mantle of Christ walking unrecognised, after his resurrection, with two of his disciples to Emmaus, whose hearts (St. Luke tells us) 'burned within' them, as he walked with them on this mystical journey.

Introduction

Gradually the hints of Christianity multiply and strengthen from poem to poem. *The Waste Land* was followed by the *The Hollow Men* with its refrain of quotations from the Lord's Prayer; *Ash Wednesday* follows and leads to Dante's famous saying, *E'n la sua volontate è nostra pace* (see Interlude, Note 3) 'In His will is our peace', which Eliot renders 'Our peace in His will'. The poem closes with a prayer:

> Suffer me not to be separated
> And let my cry come unto Thee.

The 'overwhelming question' that Prufrock had not dared to formulate was finding its answer; but the answer had not yet been digested into a play.

Eliot's first attempt at a play consists of two dazzling and often under-rated fragments called *Sweeney Agonistes*, and a whole essay could be written on the bearings of this dramatic experiment on *Murder in the Cathedral*; the subtitle calls it 'an Aristophanic melodrama', and this points not only to its farcical elements (that are combined with a kind of gruesomeness or terror) but also to its ritual character. Eliot was the first to reintroduce this ritual element into the theatre, and it plays a prominent part in *The Rock*, *Murder in the Cathedral*, *The Family Reunion*, and *The Cocktail Party*. This ritual, in Aristophanes, had its origin in long-lost Greek folk-drama, that aimed at a kind of magic to bring back the Spring; for just as a rooster believes he brings up the dawn by crowing, so men have believed that their rituals could help to bring back their necessary sun, ejecting their darkness and guilt at the end of the year, and renewing their life and light with the return of Spring. Purgation and renewal are also at the heart of Eliot's use of ritual. The ritual elements of folk-lore origin in Aristophanes were discovered and analysed in a

13

work by F. M. Cornford,[5] which greatly influenced Eliot's thought and attitude to drama, as well as his dramatic technique.

The *Sweeney* fragments are written in a vivacious jazz-rhythm, swelling to one great final serio-farcical nightmare-chorus at the end. This jazz-rhythm and use of chorus were the first signs of Eliot's effort to break up the sham-Shakespeare log-jam that had immobilised poetic drama for some three hundred years. There was a clutter of unacted and unactable plays, by all the famous names as well as by many that are now forgotten, in the pseudo-Shakespearean mould of episode and blank verse. Blake, Wordsworth, Shelley, Keats, Lamb, Byron, Tennyson,[6] and even Hardy (to mention only the most celebrated) had tried to re-enter and animate the gigantic corpse and make it write their plays for them, but with little success. It was Eliot who first saw clearly that other models must be sought, if poetry was ever to regain the stage. His choice was to fall on Aristophanes, Aeschylus, Euripides and the unknown author of *Everyman*;[7] but first on Aristophanes. In the imaginative effort of handling a new medium, the Christian theme seems to have been submerged, for the only hint of it in *Sweeney Agonistes* is given in a quotation on the title-page. It is from St. John of the Cross:

Hence the soul cannot be possessed of the divine union, until it has divested itself of the love of created beings.[8]

This aphorism may be thought the first expression of the kind of wisdom from which Eliot was to draw his conception of sanctity and his answer to Prufrock's overwhelming question. It points the way out of the suffocating wildernesses of the intellectual and material world, into the purifying wilderness of the spirit, where overwhelming answers are to be found. It is a way of denial and detachment that is a way of assertion and union, the way of the saint.

The opportunity to explore this idea further came when Eliot was invited to write the dialogue for a scenario for a pageant by Mr. E. Martin Browne, to be presented on behalf of the churches of London. This became *The Rock*, the Choruses of which described London and its suburbs as the busy centre of a desolating, meaningless, commercial activity, in which

> All our knowledge brings us nearer to our ignorance,
> All our ignorance brings us nearer to death,
> But nearness to death no nearer to God.

It is a clearer, more sermon-like picture of the life-in-death of *The Waste Land* and *Sweeney Agonistes*; and now, for the first time, is added the sharp declaration of Christian faith by which hope and meaning are given to the endless cycles of time, which without this hope and meaning

> Bring us farther from God and nearer to the dust.

It comes in the great Chorus that begins Part II of *The Rock*, telling us of the creation of the world out of waste and void, when darkness was on the face of the deep:

> Then came, at a predetermined moment, a moment in
>   time and of time,
> A moment not out of time, but in time, in what we call
>   history: transecting, bisecting the world of time,
>   a moment in time but not like a moment of time,
> A moment in time but time was made through that
>   moment: for without the meaning there is no time,
>   and that moment of time gave the meaning.
>   *(Collected Poems, Chorus VII)*

He is speaking of the Incarnation and the Rock is the rock on which Christ built his Church; it is St. Peter. He it is

15

who, at his first entry, announces the simple theme *Make perfect your will* that is later seen, in *Murder in the Cathedral*, to be the strength in Becket's action and in his passion.

We are not told, precisely, in *The Rock* what we should do to perfect our wills, save that we are to remember death and to remember God, and perpetually to rebuild His church, both in London and in our hearts, and to give thanks for His glory. The pageant ends in a ritual of prayer that sweeps the audience into an act of worship. It was written for a Christian audience on a Christian occasion.

The Chorus in *The Rock* teaches; the Chorus in *Murder in the Cathedral* learn. They are the wistful, leaderless women of Canterbury calling for spiritual guidance in their half-lived lives. They too inhabit the gloomy cycles of time; death-bringing winter, ruinous spring, disastrous summer and barren autumn make sombre their opening lament, that looks to a December happy only because in December the Son of Man was born. They need a leader, just as the builders of London churches in *The Rock* needed leaders; and the leaders are the saints, the martyrs. The idea runs on through Eliot's later work; Harry feels himself sent out into the wilderness, following 'the bright angels', at the end of *The Family Reunion*, as if taking the first step along the road of detachment and renunciation that can lead to sainthood; we are not told if he reaches it; but it is reached in martyrdom by Celia Coplestone in *The Cocktail Party*, and it is reached by Becket before our eyes.

Because he was not writing a loose chronicle play in the pseudo-Shakespearean style of Tennyson's play about Becket, Eliot offers little about the Constitutions of Clarendon or the disputed coronation ceremony which were the chief bones of contention between Becket, Henry and their continental supporters, the Pope, the Emperor and

the King of France. He is writing about a conflict between
the material and spiritual worlds and he rapidly tells us all
we need to know of the historical situation in the exposition
given by the three priests, and by the herald who announces the return of the Archbishop to the Chorus, as the
action opens. The Chorus sense a doom in which they will
find themselves involved and pray that Becket may return at
once to France; they do not wish anything to happen, they
would rather go on in the misery of their half-lived lives.

The Archbishop then enters, and in a speech of para-
doxical and somewhat abstract imagery, makes a difficult
pronouncement about the human will and its place in the
divine pattern of being, what it must suffer and how act
'that the pattern may subsist'; what Becket says to the
Chorus, as their instructor, is said to Becket at the end of
the Act by the Fourth Tempter, with a fine dramatic
irony; for Becket is to act and suffer, willing both, that the
pattern may subsist, yet cannot see (until later when light
breaks upon his understanding) how he can do either
'without perdition'; the advice he has given is turned
against him, and both paths before him—acting and
suffering—seem to 'lead to damnation in pride'. Because
the speech is difficult, it seems to need explanation, word
by word; yet, as Dr. Johnson has said, 'the easiest word,
whatever it be, can never be translated into one more
easy.'[9] It is a difficult thought:

> They know and do not know, what it is to act or suffer.
> They know and do not know, that action is suffering
> And suffering action. Neither does the agent suffer
> Nor the patient act. But both are fixed
> In an eternal action, an eternal patience
> To which all must consent that it may be willed
> And which all must suffer that they may will it,

17

> That the pattern may subsist, for the pattern is the
>   action
> And the suffering, that the wheel may turn and still
> Be for ever still.

An eternal patience is one of the key phrases, for *patience* is
the same, and not the same as *suffering*, since, like the word
passion itself, it derives from the Latin *pati*, to suffer. But
as well as the sense of suffering (enduring) there is the sense
of stillness and waitingness in *patience*; God suffers and is
still and waits in 'the perpetual struggle of Good and Evil',
to which we also are committed and in which we can only
find our peace in His will, who is at the still centre of the
wheel; we must neither act nor suffer for our own advantage, but, divested of the love of created beings, unite a will
made perfect with the will of God, to sustain the design and
pattern of perfection, to which we are called.[10] Eliot has put
his thought in another way at the end of Becket's sermon:

> A martyrdom is always made by the design of God, for
> His love of men, to warn them and to lead them, to bring
> them back to His ways. It is never the design of man; for
> the true martyr is he who has become the instrument of
> God, who has lost his will in the will of God, and who no
> longer desires anything for himself, not even the glory
> of being a martyr.

Becket must will himself to suffer a fore-ordained martyrdom and give himself to it by an action wholly free, the
action of a witness to the will of God (for the Greek word
μάρτυρ means 'witness'), not for the glory of becoming a
saint, but for the sake of uniting his will with the will of the
Love that moves the stars. And so, in the play, when he
stands on the steps to meet his murder, the four swords of
the murderers, in their ritual slaying, are the four spokes
of a wheel of which Becket is the centre—they at the

circumference, acting, he at the still centre, patient, suffering, witnessing, willing.

Eliot has followed history until the martyrdom is over; after that he abandons it and brings forward the murderer-knights to speak their bland apologies, whereas in history they stamped out of the cathedral church shouting that they were King's men. They speak prose, skipping out of their twelfth-century skins to address a twentieth-century audience in the language of political expediency of our own times. It is like a sudden series of slaps in the face and Eliot tells us it was intended to shock the audience out of their complacency.[11] It certainly succeeds; their plausibility, that has a Shavian touch in it, almost topples over into absurdity, but is under the tight control of fine parody. After they have said their pieces, they make their exit and the twelfth century resumes its hold over us in the lamentation of the First Priest and the glory of the Second; then, as in some mediaeval plays,[12] it closes in a *Te Deum* which once more sweeps both centuries together in an act of ritual worship and prayer. The pattern of sanctity has been played, and has left us involved, aware of our involvement.

The return of poetry to the stage, which is one of the revolutions that Eliot has single-handedly accomplished, has been brought about not by going back to the flower of Shakespearean style, but to the root of dramatic imagination—religion, ritual, purgation, renewal. This has meant a structural as well as a verbal poetry, a concentration upon theme that is mirrored in the intensity of the situation itself. Based upon history, it is a distillation of it, a particular image of a perpetual situation, the witnessing to what is to be rendered to God when Caesar stakes his ever-encroaching claims; against which even Lazarus come from the dead would not be listened to. It needs the human part in sainthood, purified into a willing harmony with the Will at the still centre of things. A vision of this kind, seen working itself out through the actualities of history, is what makes *Murder in the Cathedral* poetry; the ritualised form, the verbal imagery, the varying flow of metrical rhythm, all issue from this creative or poetic concentration upon a theme seen in singleness; though it is presented in terms of the twelfth century, it comprehends and answers problems that seem quintessentially those of Prufrock and the Waste Lands of the twentieth.

NOTE ON THIS EDITION

When Mr. Eliot invited me to prepare this edition I called on him to ask if there were any particular points he would like me to stress in it. He replied that he would like me to show how the action and dialogue were based in authentic contemporary records and were faithful to historical truth. He also asked me to illustrate the derivation of the verse from *Everyman*. 'The versification is important to me,' he said. Speaking of the choruses, he approved of occasionally dividing them, by giving paragraphs or even sentences to smaller groups or to individual speakers, to 'give the effect of emotionally excited women under a great fear. The feeling of terror in their queer visions is more important than the precise meaning'. Speaking of the Tempter-Knights, he remarked 'They represent the persuasiveness of evil'; he added that their apology in Part II should not be played as if they were drunk, though 'possibly the youngest may have had a drink or two, because he was shy'. The apology was on no account to be treated as a joke.

When I had completed my Introduction I sent it to Mr. Eliot, who gave it his full approval. The Notes and Appendices were, unhappily, not completed until after he had entered upon his last illness: he consequently never saw them.

MURDER IN THE CATHEDRAL

Part I

*

Characters

A CHORUS OF WOMEN OF CANTERBURY
THREE PRIESTS OF THE CATHEDRAL
A MESSENGER
ARCHBISHOP THOMAS BECKET
FOUR TEMPTERS
ATTENDANTS

*The Scene is the Archbishop's Hall,
on December 2nd, 1170*

Here let us, stand, close by the cathedral. Here let us
  wait.
Are we drawn by danger?[1] Is it the knowledge of safety,
  that draws our feet
Towards the cathedral? What danger can be
For us, the poor, the poor women of Canterbury? what
  tribulation
With which we are not already familiar? There is no
  danger
For us, and there is no safety in the cathedral. Some pre-
  sage of an act
Which our eyes are compelled to witness, has forced our feet
Towards the cathedral. We are forced to bear witness.[2]

Since golden October[3] declined into sombre November
And the apples were gathered and stored, and the land be- 10
  came brown sharp points of death in a waste of water
  and mud,
The New Year waits, breathes, waits, whispers in darkness.
While the labourer kicks off a muddy boot and stretches his
  hand to the fire,
The New Year waits, destiny waits for the coming.
Who has stretched out his hand to the fire[4] and remem-
  bered the Saints at All Hallows,
Remembered the martyrs and saints who wait? and who
  shall
Stretch out his hand to the fire, and deny his master? who
  shall be warm
By the fire, and deny his master?

Seven years[5] and the summer is over
Seven years since the Archbishop left us,
20 He who was always kind to his people.
But it would not be well if he should return.
King rules or barons rule;
We have suffered various oppression,
But mostly we are left to our own devices,
And we are content if we are left alone.
We try to keep our households in order;
The merchant, shy and cautious, tries to compile a little
    fortune,
And the labourer bends to his piece of earth, earth-
    colour, his own colour.
Preferring to pass unobserved.
30 Now I fear disturbance of the quiet seasons:
Winter shall come bringing death from the sea,[6]
Ruinous spring shall beat at our doors,
Root and shoot shall eat our eyes and our ears,
Disastrous summer burn up the beds of our streams
And the poor shall wait for another decaying October.
Why should the summer bring consolation
For autumn fires and winter fogs?
What shall we do in the heat of summer
But wait in barren orchards for another October?
40 Some malady is coming upon us. We wait, we wait,
And the saints and martyrs wait, for those who shall be
    martyrs and saints.
Destinywaitsinthehandof God,shapingthestillunshapen:
I have seen these things in a shaft of sunlight.
Destiny waits in the hand of God, not in the hands of
    statesmen
Who do, some well, some ill, planning and guessing,
Having their aims which turn in their hands in the pattern
    of time.

Come, happy December,[7] who shall observe you, who shall
    preserve you?
Shall the Son of Man be born again in the litter of scorn?
For us, the poor, there is no action,
But only to wait and to witness.   50
[*Enter* PRIESTS.]

FIRST PRIEST

Seven years and the summer is over.
Seven years since the Archbishop left us.

SECOND PRIEST

What does the Archbishop do, and our Sovereign Lord the
    Pope
With the stubborn King and the French King
In ceaseless intrigue, combinations,
In conference, meetings accepted, meetings refused,
Meetings unended or endless
At one place or another in France?

THIRD PRIEST

I see nothing quite conclusive in the art of temporal govern-
    ment,
But violence, duplicity and frequent malversation.[8]   60
King rules or barons rule:
The strong man strongly and the weak man by caprice.
They have but one law, to seize the power and keep it,
And the steadfast can manipulate the greed and lust of
    others,
The feeble is devoured by his own.

FIRST PRIEST

Shall these things not end
Until the poor at the gate

Have forgotten their friend, their Father in God, have for-
    gotten
That they had a friend?
[*Enter* MESSENGER.]

MESSENGER

70 Servants of God, and watchers of the temple,
  I am here to inform you, without circumlocution:
  The Archbishop is in England, and is close outside the city.
  I was sent before in haste
  To give you notice of his coming, as much as was possible,
  That you may prepare to meet him.

FIRST PRIEST

What, is the exile ended, is our Lord Archbishop
  Reunited with the King? what reconciliation
  Of two proud men?

THIRD PRIEST
               What peace can be found
To grow between the hammer and the anvil?

SECOND PRIEST
                         Tell us,
80 Are the old disputes at an end, is the wall of pride cast down
  That divided them? Is it peace or war?

FIRST PRIEST
                    Does he come
In full assurance, or only secure
  In the power of Rome, the spiritual rule,
  The assurance of right, and the love of the people?

MESSENGER

You are right to express a certain incredulity.
He comes in pride and sorrow, affirming all his claims,
Assured, beyond doubt, of the devotion of the people,
Who receive him with scenes of frenzied enthusiasm,[9]
Lining the road and throwing down their capes,
Strewing the way with leaves and late flowers of the season.   90
The streets of the city will be packed to suffocation,
And I think that his horse will be deprived of its tail,[10]
A single hair of which becomes a precious relic.
He is at one with the Pope, and with the King of France,
Who indeed would have liked to detain him in his kingdom:
But as for our King, that is another matter.

FIRST PRIEST

But again, is it war or peace?

MESSENGER

                    Peace, but not the kiss of peace.[11]
A patched up affair, if you ask my opinion.
And if you ask me, I think the Lord Archbishop
Is not the man to cherish any illusions,   100
Or yet to diminish the least of his pretensions.
If you ask my opinion, I think that this peace
Is nothing like an end, or like a beginning.
It is common knowledge that when the Archbishop
Parted from the King, he said to the King,
My Lord, he said, I leave you as a man[12]
Whom in this life I shall not see again.
I have this, I assure you, on the highest authority;
There are several opinions as to what he meant,
But no one considers it a happy prognostic.   110

[*Exit.*]

27

FIRST PRIEST

I fear for the Archbishop, I fear for the Church,
I know that the pride bred of sudden prosperity
Was but confirmed by a bitter adversity.
I saw him as Chancellor, flattered by the King,
Liked or feared by courtiers, in their overbearing fashion,
Despised and despising, always isolated,
Never one among them, always insecure;
His pride always feeding upon his own virtues,
Pride drawing sustenance from impartiality,
120 Pride drawing sustenance from generosity,
Loathing power given by temporal devolution,[13]
Wishing subjection to God alone.
Had the King been greater, or had he been weaker
Things had perhaps been different for Thomas.

SECOND PRIEST

Yet our lord is returned. Our lord has come back to his own
    again.
We have had enough of waiting, from December to dismal
    December.
The Archbishop shall be at our head, dispelling dismay and
    doubt.
He will tell us what we are to do, he will give us our orders,
    instruct us.
Our Lord is at one with the Pope, and also the King of France.
130 We can lean on a rock, we can feel a firm foothold
Against the perpetual wash of tides of balance of forces of
    barons and landholders.
The rock of God is beneath our feet. Let us meet the Arch-
    bishop with cordial thanksgiving:
Our lord, our Archbishop returns. And when the Arch-
    bishop returns

Our doubts are dispelled. Let us therefore rejoice,
I say rejoice, and show a glad face for his welcome.
I am the Archbishop's man.[14] Let us give the Archbishop
    welcome!

THIRD PRIEST

For good or ill, let the wheel turn.
The wheel has been still, these seven years, and no good.
For ill or good, let the wheel turn.
For who knows the end of good or evil?   140
Until the grinders cease[15]
And the door shall be shut in the street,
And all the daughters of music shall be brought low.

CHORUS

Here is no continuing city,[16] here is no abiding stay.
Ill the wind, ill the time, uncertain the profit, certain the
    danger.
O late late late, late is the time, late too late, and rotten the
    year;
Evil the wind, and bitter the sea, and grey the sky, grey
    grey grey.
O Thomas, return, Archbishop; return, return to France.
Return. Quickly. Quietly. Leave us to perish in quiet.
You come with applause, you come with rejoicing, but you
    come bringing death into Canterbury:[17]   150
A doom on the house, a doom on yourself, a doom on the
    world.

We do not wish anything to happen.
Seven years we have lived quietly.
Succeeded in avoiding notice,
Living and partly living.[18]
There have been oppression and luxury,
There have been poverty and licence,

There has been minor injustice,
Yet we have gone on living,
160 Living and partly living.
Sometimes the corn has failed us,
Sometimes the harvest is good,
One year is a year of rain,
Another a year of dryness,
One year the apples are abundant,
Another year the plums are lacking.
Yet we have gone on living,
Living and partly living.
We have kept the feasts, heard the masses,
170 We have brewed beer and cyder,
Gathered wood against the winter,
Talked at the corner of the fire,
Talked at the corners of streets,
Talked not always in whispers,
Living and partly living.
We have seen births, deaths and marriages,
We have had various scandals,
We have been afflicted with taxes,
We have had laughter and gossip,
180 Several girls have disappeared
Unaccountably, and some not able to.
We have all had our private terrors,
Our particular shadows, our secret fears.
But now a great fear is upon us, a fear not of one but of many,
A fear like birth and death, when we see birth and death
    alone
In a void apart. We
Are afraid in a fear which we cannot know, which we cannot
    face, which none understands,
And our hearts are torn from us, our brains unskinned like
    the layers of an onion, our selves are lost lost

In a final fear which none understands. O Thomas Arch-
    bishop,
O Thomas our Lord, leave us and leave us be, in our humble 190
    and tarnished frame of existence, leave us; do not ask
    us
To stand to the doom on the house, the doom on the Arch-
    bishop, the doom on the world.
Archbishop, secure and assured of your fate, unaffrayed[19]
    among the shades, do you realise what you ask, do you
    realise what it means
To the small folk drawn into the pattern of fate, the small
    folk who live among small things,
The strain on the brain of the small folk who stand to the
    doom of the house, the doom of their lord, the doom of
    the world?
O Thomas, Archbishop, leave us, leave us, leave sullen
    Dover, and set sail for France. Thomas our Archbishop
    still our Archbishop even in France. Thomas Arch-
    bishop, set the white sail between the grey sky and the
    bitter sea, leave us, leave us for France.

SECOND PRIEST

What a way to talk at such a juncture!
You are foolish, immodest and babbling women.
Do you not know that the good Archbishop
Is likely to arrive at any moment?
The crowds in the streets will be cheering and cheering, 200
You go on croaking like frogs in the treetops:
But frogs at least can be cooked and eaten.
Whatever you are afraid of, in your craven apprehension,
Let me ask you at the least to put on pleasant faces,
And give a hearty welcome to our good Archbishop.
[*Enter* THOMAS.]

THOMAS

Peace. And let them be, in their exaltation.
They speak better than they know, and beyond your under-
        standing.
They know and do not know,[20] what it is to act or suffer.
They know and do not know, that action is suffering
210 And suffering is action. Neither does the agent suffer
Nor the patient act. But both are fixed
In an eternal action, an eternal patience
To which all must consent that it may be willed
And which all must suffer that they may will it,
That the pattern may subsist, for the pattern is the action
And the suffering, that the wheel may turn and still
Be forever still.

SECOND PRIEST

O my Lord, forgive me, I did not see you coming,
Engrossed by the chatter of these foolish women.
220 Forgive us, my Lord, you would have had a better welcome
If we had been sooner prepared for the event.
But your Lordship knows that seven years of waiting,
Seven years of prayer, seven years of emptiness,
Have better prepared our hearts for your coming,
Than seven days could make ready Canterbury.
However, I will have fires laid in all your rooms
To take the chill off our English December,
Your Lordship now being used to a better climate.
Your Lordship will find your rooms in order as you left them.

THOMAS

230 And will try to leave them in order as I find them.
I am more than grateful for all your kind attentions.
These are small matters. Little rest in Canterbury
With eager enemies restless about us.

Rebellious bishops,[21] York, London, Salisbury,
Would have intercepted our letters,
Filled the coast with spies and sent to meet me
Some who hold me in bitterest hate.
By God's grace aware of their prevision
I sent my letters on another day,
Had fair crossing, found at Sandwich   240
Broc, Warenne, and the Sheriff of Kent,[22]
Those who had sworn to have my head from me
Only John, the Dean of Salisbury,[23]
Fearing for the King's name, warning against treason,
Made them hold their hands. So for the time
We are unmolested.

FIRST PRIEST
But do they follow after?

THOMAS
For a little time the hungry hawk
Will only soar and hover, circling lower,
Waiting excuse, pretence, opportunity.
End will be simple, sudden, God-given.   250
Meanwhile the substance of our first act
Will be shadows, and the strife with shadows.
Heavier the interval than the consummation.
All things prepare the event. Watch.
[*Enter* FIRST TEMPTER.]

FIRST TEMPTER[24]
You see, my Lord, I do not wait upon ceremony:
Here I have come, forgetting all acrimony,
Hoping that your present gravity
Will find excuse for my humble levity
Remembering all the good time past.

260 Your Lordship won't despise an old friend out of favour?
Old Tom, gay Tom, Becket of London,
Your Lordship won't forget that evening on the river
When the King and you and I were all friends together?
Friendship should be more than biting Time can sever.
What, my Lord, now that you recover[25]
Favour with the King, shall we say that summer's over
Or that the good time cannot last?
Fluting in the meadows, viols in the hall,
Laughter and apple-blossom floating on the water,
270 Singing at nightfall, whispering in chambers,
Fires devouring the winter season,
Eating up the darkness, with wit and wine and wisdom!
Now that the King and you are in amity,
Clergy and laity may return to gaiety,
Mirth and sportfulness need not walk warily.

THOMAS
You talk of seasons that are past. I remember:
Not worth forgetting.

TEMPTER
And of the new season.
Spring has come in winter. Snow in the branches
Shall float as sweet as blossoms. Ice along the ditches
280 Mirror the sunlight. Love in the orchard
Send the sap shooting. Mirth matches melancholy.

THOMAS
We do not know very much of the future
Except that from generation to generation
The same things happen again and again.
Men learn little from others' experience.
But in the life of one man, never

34

The same time returns. Sever
The cord, shed the scale. Only
The fool, fixed in his folly, may think
He can turn the wheel on which he turns.[26]   290

TEMPTER

My Lord, a nod is as good as a wink.
A man will often love what he spurns.
For the good times past, that are come again
I am your man.

THOMAS
                      Not in this train.
Look to your behaviour. You were safer
Think of penitence and follow your master.[27]

TEMPTER

Not at this gait!
If you go so fast, others may go faster.
Your Lordship is too proud!
The safest beast is not the one that roars most loud.   300
This was not the way of the King our master!
You were not used to be so hard upon sinners
When they were your friends. Be easy, man!
The easy man lives to eat the best dinners.
Take a friend's advice. Leave well alone,
Or your goose may be cooked and eaten to the bone.

THOMAS

You come twenty years too late.

TEMPTER

Then I leave you to your fate.
I leave you to the pleasures of your higher vices,

310   Which will have to be paid for at higher prices.
      Farewell, my Lord, I do not wait upon ceremony,
      I leave as I came, forgetting all acrimony,
      Hoping that your present gravity
      Will find excuse for my humble levity.
      If you will remember me, my Lord, at your prayers,
      I'll remember you at kissing-time below the stairs.

THOMAS

      Leave-well-alone, the springtime fancy,
      So one thought goes whistling down the wind.
      The impossible is still temptation.[28]
320   The impossible, the undersirable,
      Voices under sleep, waking a dead world,
      So that the mind may not be whole in the present.
      [*Enter* SECOND TEMPTER.]

SECOND TEMPTER

      Your Lordship has forgotten me, perhaps. I will remind you.
      We met at Clarendon, at Northampton,[29]
      And last at Montmirail, in Maine. Now that I have recalled
          them,
      Let us but set these not too pleasant memories
      In balance against each other, earlier
      And weightier ones: those of the Chancellorship.
      See how the late ones rise![30] You, master of policy
330   Whom all acknowledged, should guide the state again.

THOMAS

      Your meaning?

TEMPTER

      The Chancellorship that you resigned
      When you were made Archbishop—that was a mistake

On your part—still may be regained. Think, my Lord,
Power obtained grows to glory,
Life lasting, a permanent possession.
A templed tomb, monument of marble.
Rule over men reckon no madness.

THOMAS
To the man of God what gladness?

TEMPTER
                                    Sadness
Only to those giving love to God alone.
Shall he who held the solid substance   340
Wander waking with deceitful shadows?[31]
Power is present. Holiness hereafter.

THOMAS
    Who then?

TEMPTER
    The Chancellor. King and Chancellor.
King commands. Chancellor richly rules.
This is a sentence[32] not taught in the schools.
To set down the great, protect the poor,
Beneath the throne of God can man do more?
Disarm the ruffian, strengthen the laws,
Rule for the good of the better cause,
Dispensing justice make all even,   350
Is thrive on earth, and perhaps in heaven.

THOMAS
What means?

TEMPTER
Real power
Is purchased at price of a certain submission.
Your spiritual power is earthly perdition.
Power is present, for him who will wield.

THOMAS
Who shall have it?[33]

TEMPTER
He who will come.

THOMAS
What shall be the month?

TEMPTER
The last from the first.

THOMAS
What shall we give for it?

TEMPTER
Pretence of priestly power.

THOMAS
Why should we give it?

TEMPTER
For the power and the glory.

THOMAS
360 No!

TEMPTER
Yes! Or bravery will be broken,
Cabined in Canterbury, realmless ruler,
Self-bound servant of a powerless Pope,
The old stag, circled with hounds.

THOMAS
No!

TEMPTER
Yes! men must manœuvre. Monarchs also,
Waging war abroad, need fast friends at home.
Private policy is a public profit;
Dignity still shall be dressed with decorum.

THOMAS
You forget the bishops[34]
Whom I have laid under excommunication.

TEMPTER
Hungry hatred   370
Will not strive against intelligent self-interest.

THOMAS
You forget the barons. Who will not forget
Constant curbing of petty privilege.

TEMPTER
Against the barons
Is King's cause, churl's cause, Chancellor's cause.

THOMAS
No! shall I, who keep the keys
Of heaven and hell, supreme alone in England,

Who bind and loose,[35] with power from the Pope,
Descend to desire a punier power?
380 Delegate to deal the doom of damnation,
To condemn kings, not serve among their servants,
Is my open office. No! Go.

TEMPTER

Then I leave you to your fate.
Your sin soars sunward, covering kings' falcons.[36]

THOMAS

Temporal power, to build a good world,
To keep order, as the world knows order.
Those who put their faith in worldly order
Not controlled by the order of God,
In confident ignorance, but arrest disorder,[37]
390 Make it fast,[38] breed fatal disease,
Degrade what they exalt. Power with the King—
I *was* the King, his arm, his better reason.
But what was once exaltation
Would now only be mean descent.
[*Enter* THIRD TEMPTER.]

THIRD TEMPTER

I am an unexpected visitor.

THOMAS
I expected you.

TEMPTER

But not in this guise, or for my present purpose.

THOMAS

No purpose brings surprise.

TEMPTER
                    Well, my Lord
I am no trifler, and no politician.
To idle or intrigue at court
I have no skill. I am no courtier.   400
I know a horse, a dog, a wench;
I know how to hold my estates in order,
A country-keeping lord who minds his own business.
It is we country lords who know the country
And we who know what the country needs.
It is our country. We care for the country.
We are the backbone of the nation.
We, not the plotting parasites
About the King. Excuse my bluntness:
I am a rough straightforward Englishman.   410

THOMAS
Proceed straight forward.

TEMPTER
                    Purpose is plain.
Endurance of friendship does not depend
Upon ourselves, but upon circumstance.
But circumstance is not undetermined.
Unreal friendship may turn to real
But real friendship, once ended, cannot be mended.
Sooner shall enmity turn to alliance.
The enmity that never knew friendship
Can sooner know accord.

THOMAS
                    For a countryman
You wrap your meaning in as dark generality   420
As any courtier.

TEMPTER
This is the simple fact!
You have no hope of reconciliation
With Henry the King. You look only
To blind assertion in isolation.
That is a mistake.

THOMAS
O Henry, O my King!

TEMPTER
Other friends
May be found in the present situation.
King in England is not all-powerful;
King is in France, squabbling in Anjou;
Round him waiting hungry sons.
430 We are for England. We are in England.
You and I, my Lord, are Normans.[39]
England is a land for Norman
Sovereignty. Let the Angevin[40]
Destroy himself, fighting in Anjou.
He does not understand us, the English barons.
We are the people.

THOMAS
To what does this lead?

TEMPTER
To a happy coalition
Of intelligent interests.

THOMAS
But what have you—
If you do speak for barons—

TEMPTER
                    For a powerful party
Which has turned its eyes in your direction—   440
To gain from you, your Lordship asks.
For us, Church favour would be an advantage,
Blessing of Pope powerful protection
In the fight for liberty. You, my Lord,
In being with us, would fight a good stroke
At once, for England and for Rome,
Ending the tyrannous jurisdiction[41]
Of king's court over bishop's court,
Of king's court over baron's court.

THOMAS
Which I helped to found.   450

TEMPTER
                    Which you helped to found.
But time past is time forgotten.
We expect the rise of a new constellation.

THOMAS
And if the Archbishop cannot trust the King,
How can he trust those who work for King's undoing?

TEMPTER
Kings will allow no power but their own;
Church and people have good cause against the throne.

THOMAS
If the Archbishop cannot trust the Throne,
He has good cause to trust none but God alone.
I ruled once as Chancellor
And men like you were glad to wait at my door.   460

Not only in the court, but in the field
And in the tilt-yard[42] I made many yield.
Shall I who ruled like an eagle over doves
Now take the shape of a wolf among wolves?
Pursue your treacheries as you have done before:
No one shall say that I betrayed a king.

TEMPTER

Then, my Lord, I shall not wait at your door.
And I well hope, before another spring
The King will show his regard for your loyalty.

THOMAS

470 To make, then break,[43] this thought has come before,
The desperate exercise of failing power.
Samson in Gaza did no more.
But if I break, I must break myself alone.
[*Enter* FOURTH TEMPTER.]

FOURTH TEMPTER

Well done, Thomas, your will is hard to bend.
And with me beside you, you shall not lack a friend.

THOMAS

Who are you?[44] I expected
Three visitors, not four.

TEMPTER

Do not be surprised to receive one more.
Had I been expected, I had been here before.
480 I always precede expectation.

THOMAS

          Who are you?

TEMPTER

As you do not know me, I do not need a name,
And, as you know me, that is why I come.
You know me, but have never seen my face.
To meet before was never time or place.

THOMAS

Say what you come to say.

TEMPTER
                    It shall be said at last.
Hooks have been baited with morsels of the past.[45]
Wantonness is weakness. As for the King,
His hardened hatred shall have no end.
You know truly, the King will never trust
Twice, the man who has been his friend.   490
Borrow use cautiously, employ
Your services as long as you have to lend.
You would wait for trap to snap
Having served your turn, broken and crushed.
As for barons, envy of lesser men
Is still more stubborn than king's anger.
Kings have public policy, barons private profit,
Jealousy raging possession of the fiend.
Barons are employable against each other;
Greater enemies must kings destroy.   500

THOMAS

What is your counsel?

TEMPTER
                    Fare forward to the end.
All other ways are closed to you
Except the way already chosen.

                    45

But what is pleasure, kingly rule,
Or rule of men beneath a king,
With craft in corners, stealthy stratagem,
To general grasp of spiritual power?
Man oppressed by sin, since Adam fell—
You hold the keys of heaven and hell.
510 Power to bind and loose: bind, Thomas, bind,
King and bishop under your heel.
King, emperor, bishop, baron, king:
Uncertain mastery of melting armies,
War, plague, and revolution,
New conspiracies, broken pacts;
To be master or servant within an hour,
This is the course of temporal power.
The Old King[46] shall know it, when at last breath,
No sons, no empire, he bites broken teeth.
520 You hold the skein: wind, Thomas, wind
The thread of eternal life and death.
You hold this power, hold it.

THOMAS
         Supreme, in this land?

TEMPTER
Supreme, but for one.[47]

THOMAS
         That I do not understand.

TEMPTER
It is not for me to tell you how this may be so;
I am only here, Thomas, to tell you what you know.

THOMAS
How long shall this be?

TEMPTER

Save what you know already, ask nothing of me.
But think, Thomas, think of glory after death.
When king is dead, there's another king,
And one more king is another reign.   530
King is forgotten, when another shall come:
Saint and Martyr rule from the tomb.
Think, Thomas, think of enemies dismayed,
Creeping in penance, frightened of a shade;
Think of pilgrims, standing in line
Before the glittering jewelled shrine,
From generation to generation
Bending the knee in supplication,
Think of the miracles, by God's grace,
And think of your enemies, in another place.   540

THOMAS

I have thought of these things.

TEMPTER

                              That is why I tell you.
Your thoughts have more power than kings to compel you.
You have also thought, sometimes at your prayers,
Sometimes hesitating at the angles of stairs,[48]
And between sleep and waking, early in the morning,
When the bird cries, have thought of further scorning,
That nothing lasts, but the wheel turns,
The nest is rifled, and the bird mourns;
That the shrine shall be pillaged,[49] and the gold spent,
The jewels gone for light ladies' ornament,   550
The sanctuary broken, and its stores
Swept into the laps of parasites and whores.
When miracles cease, and the faithful desert you.
And men shall only do their best to forget you.

And later is worse, when men will not hate you
Enough to defame or to execrate you,
But pondering the qualities that you lacked
Will only try to find the historical fact.
When men shall declare that there was no mystery
560 About this man who played a certain part in history.

THOMAS

But what is there to do? what is left to be done?
Is there no enduring crown to be won?

TEMPTER

Yes, Thomas, yes; you have thought of that too.
What can compare with glory of Saints
Dwelling forever in presence of God?
What earthly glory, of king or emperor,
What earthly pride, that is not poverty
Compared with richness of heavenly grandeur?
Seek the way of martyrdom, make yourself the lowest
570 On earth, to be high in heaven.
And see far off below you, where the gulf is fixed,
Your persecutors, in timeless torment,
Parched passion, beyond expiation.

THOMAS
                              No!
Who are you, tempting with my own desires?
Others have come, temporal tempters,
With pleasure and power at palpable price.
What do you offer? what do you ask?

TEMPTER

I offer what you desire. I ask
What you have to give. Is it too much
580 For such a vision of eternal grandeur?

48

THOMAS

Others offered real goods, worthless
But real. You only offer
Dreams to damnation.

TEMPTER

You have often dreamt them.

THOMAS

Is there no way, in my soul's sickness,
Does not lead to damnation in pride?
I well know that these temptations
Mean present vanity and future torment.
Can sinful pride be driven out
Only by more sinful? Can I neither act nor suffer[50]
Without perdition?   590

TEMPTER

You know and do not know, what it is to act or suffer.
You know and do not know, that action is suffering,
And suffering action. Neither does the agent suffer
Nor the patient act. But both are fixed
In an eternal action, an eternal patience
To which all must consent that it may be willed
And which all must suffer that they may will it,
That the pattern may subsist, that the wheel may turn and
    still
Be forever still.

CHORUS

There is no rest in the house. There is no rest in the street. 600
I hear restless movement of feet. And the air is heavy and
    thick.
Thick and heavy the sky. And the earth presses up against
    our feet.

What is the sickly smell, the vapour? the dark green light
    from a cloud on a withered tree? The earth is heaving
    to parturition of issue of hell. What is the sticky dew
    that forms on the back of my hand?

THE FOUR TEMPTERS

Man's life is a cheat and a disappointment;
All things are unreal,
Unreal or disappointing:
The Catherine wheel, the pantomime cat,[51]
The prizes given at the children's party,
The prize awarded for the English Essay,
610 The scholar's degree, the statesman's decoration.
All things become less real, man passes
From unreality to unreality.
This man is obstinate, blind, intent
On self-destruction,
Passing from deception to deception,
From grandeur to grandeur to final illusion,
Lost in the wonder of his own greatness,
The enemy of society, enemy of himself.

THE THREE PRIESTS

O Thomas my Lord do not fight the intractable tide,
620 Do not sail the irresistible wind; in the storm,
Should we not wait for the sea to subside, in the night
Abide the coming of day, when the traveller may find his
    way,
The sailor lay course by the sun?

CHORUS, PRIESTS *and* TEMPTERS *alternately*

C. Is it the owl that calls,[52] or a signal between the trees?
P. Is the window-bar made fast, is the door under lock and
      bolt?

T. Is it rain that taps at the window, is it wind that pokes
         at the door?

C. Does the torch flame in the hall, the candle in the room?

P. Does the watchman walk by the wall?

T. Does the mastiff prowl by the gate?

C. Death has a hundred hands and walks by a thousand   630
         ways.

P. He may come in the sight of all, he may pass unseen
         unheard.

T. Come whispering through the ear, or a sudden shock on
         the skull.

C. A man may walk with a lamp at night, and yet be
         drowned in a ditch.

P. A man may climb the stair in the day, and slip on a
         broken step.

T. A man may sit at meat, and feel the cold in his groin.

CHORUS

We have not been happy, my Lord, we have not been too
    happy.

We are not ignorant women, we know what we must expect
    and not expect.

We know of oppression and torture,[53]

We know of extortion and violence,

Destitution, disease,   640

The old without fire in winter,

The child without milk in summer,

Our labour taken away from us,

Our sins made heavier upon us.

We have seen the young man mutilated,

The torn girl trembling by the mill-stream.

And meanwhile we have gone on living,

Living and partly living,

Picking together the pieces,

51

650 Gathering faggots at nightfall,
Building a partial shelter,
For sleeping, and eating and drinking and laughter.

God gave us always some reason, some hope; but now a
new terror has soiled us, which none can avert, none
can avoid, flowing under our feet and over the sky;
Under doors and down chimneys, flowing in at the ear and
the mouth and the eye.
God is leaving us, God is leaving us, more pang, more pain
than birth or death.
Sweet and cloying through the dark air
Falls the stifling scent of despair;
The forms take shape in the dark air:
Puss-purr of leopard,[54] footfall of padding bear,
660 Palm-pat of nodding ape, square hyaena waiting
For laughter, laughter, laughter. The Lords of Hell are here.
They curl round you, lie at your feet, swing and wing
through the dark air.
O Thomas Archbishop, save us, save us, save yourself that
we may be saved;
Destroy yourself and we are destroyed.

THOMAS

Now is my way clear, now is the meaning plain;
Temptation shall not come in this kind again.
The last temptation is the greatest treason:
To do the right deed for the wrong reason.
The natural vigour in the venial sin[55]
670 Is the way in which our lives begin.
Thirty years ago, I searched all the ways[56]
That lead to pleasure, advancement and praise.
Delight in sense, in learning and in thought,
Music and philosophy, curiosity,
The purple bullfinch in the lilac tree,

The tilt-yard skill, the strategy of chess,
Love in the garden, singing to the instrument,
Were all things equally desirable.
Ambition comes when early force is spent
And when we find no longer all things possible.   680
Ambition comes behind and unobservable.
Sin grows with doing good. When I imposed the King's law
In England, and waged war with him against Toulouse,
I beat the barons at their own game. I
Could then despise the men who thought me most con-
      temptible,
The raw nobility, whose manners matched their fingernails.
While I ate out of the King's dish
To become servant of God was never my wish.
Servant of God has chance of greater sin
And sorrow, than the man who serves a king.   690
For those who serve the greater cause may make the cause
      serve them,
Still doing right: and striving with political men
May make that cause political, not by what they do
But by what they are. I know
What yet remains to show you of my history
Will seem to most of you at best futility,
Senseless self-slaughter of a lunatic,
Arrogant passion of a fanatic.
I know that history at all times draws
The strangest consequence from remotest cause.   700
But for every evil, every sacrilege,
Crime, wrong, oppression and the axe's edge,
Indifference, exploitation, you, and you,
And you, must all be punished. So must you.
I shall no longer act or suffer, to the sword's end.
Now my good Angel, whom God appoints
To be my guardian, hover over the swords' points.

INTERLUDE

'Glory to God in the highest,[1] and on earth peace to men of good will.' *The fourteenth verse of the second chapter of the Gospel according to Saint Luke.* In the Name of the Father, and of the Son, and of the Holy Ghost. Amen.

Dear children of God, my sermon this Christmas morning will be a very short one. I wish only that you should meditate in your hearts the deep meaning and mystery of our masses of Christmas Day. For whenever Mass is said, we re-enact the Passion and Death of Our Lord; and on this Christmas Day we do this in celebration of His Birth. So that at the same moment we rejoice in His coming for the salvation of men, and offer again to God His Body and Blood in sacrifice, oblation and satisfaction for the sins of the whole world. It was in this same night that has just passed, that a 10 multitude of the heavenly host appeared before the shepherds at Bethlehem, saying 'Glory to God in the highest, and on earth peace to men of good will'; at this same time of all the year that we celebrate at once the Birth of Our Lord and His Passion and Death upon the Cross. Beloved, as the World sees, this is to behave in a strange fashion. For who in the World will both mourn and rejoice at once and for the same reason? For either joy will be overborne by mourning, or mourning will be cast out by joy; so it is only in these our Christian mysteries that we can rejoice and 20 mourn at once for the same reason. Now think for a moment about the meaning of this word 'peace'. Does it seem strange

to you that the angels should have announced Peace, when
ceaselessly the world has been stricken with War and the
fear of War? Does it seem to you that the angelic voices
were mistaken, and that the promise was a disappointment
and a cheat?

Reflect now, how Our Lord Himself spoke of Peace. He
said to His disciples, 'Peace I leave with you, my peace I
30 give unto you.'[2] Did He mean peace as we think of it: the
kingdom of England at peace with its neighbours, the
barons at peace with the King, the householder counting
over his peaceful gains, the swept hearth, his best wine for
a friend at the table, his wife singing to the children? Those
men His disciples knew no such things: they went forth to
journey afar, to suffer by land and sea, to know torture, imprisonment, disappointment, to suffer death by martyrdom.
What then did He mean? If you ask that, remember then
that He said also, 'Not as the world gives, give I unto you.'
40 So then, He gave to His disciples peace, but not peace as
the world gives.

Consider also one thing of which you have probably never
thought. Not only do we at the feast of Christmas celebrate
at once our Lord's Birth and His Death: but on the next
day we celebrate the martyrdom of His first martyr, the
blessed Stephen. Is it an accident, do you think, that the
day of the first martyr follows immediately the day of the
Birth of Christ? By no means. Just as we rejoice and mourn
at once, in the Birth and in the Passion of Our Lord; so also,
50 in a smaller figure, we both rejoice and mourn in the death
of martyrs. We mourn, for the sins of the world that has
martyred them; we rejoice, that another soul is numbered
among the Saints in Heaven, for the glory of God and for
the salvation of men.

Beloved, we do not think of a martyr simply as a good
Christian who has been killed because he is a Christian: for

that would be solely to mourn. We do not think of him simply as a good Christian who has been elevated to the company of the Saints: for that would be simply to rejoice: and neither our mourning nor our rejoicing is as the world's is. A Christian martyrdom is never an accident, for Saints are not made by accident. Still less is a Christian martyrdom the effect of a man's will to become a Saint, as a man by willing and contriving may become a ruler of men. A martyrdom is always the design of God, for His love of men, to warn them and to lead them, to bring them back to His ways. It is never the design of man; for the true martyr is he who has become the instrument of God, who has lost his will in the will of God,[3] and who no longer desires anything for himself, not even the glory of being a martyr. So thus as on earth the Church mourns and rejoices at once, in a fashion that the world cannot understand; so in Heaven the Saints are most high, having made themselves most low, and are seen, not as we see them, but in the light of the Godhead from which they draw their being.

I have spoken to you to-day, dear children of God, of the martyrs of the past, asking you to remember especially our martyr of Canterbury, the blessed Archbishop Elphege;[4] because it is fitting, on Christ's birth day, to remember what is that Peace which He brought; and because, dear children, I do not think I shall ever preach to you again; and because it is possible that in a short time you may have yet another martyr, and that one perhaps not the last. I would have you keep in your hearts these words that I say, and think of them at another time. In the Name of the Father, and of the Son, and of the Holy Ghost. Amen.

Part II

*

Characters

THREE PRIESTS
FOUR KNIGHTS
ARCHBISHOP THOMAS BECKET
CHORUS OF WOMEN OF CANTERBURY
ATTENDANTS

*The first scene is in the Archbishop's Hall,
the second scene is in the Cathedral,
on December 29th, 1170*

CHORUS

Does the bird sing in the South?
Only the sea-bird cries, driven inland by the storm.
What sign of the spring of the year?
Only the death of the old: not a stir, not a shoot, not a
    breath.
Do the days begin to lengthen?
Longer and darker the day, shorter and colder the night.
Still and stifling the air: but a wind is stored up in the East.
The starved crow sits in the field, attentive; and in the
    wood
The owl rehearses the hollow note of death.
What signs of a bitter spring?   10
The wind stored up in the East.
What, at the time of the birth of Our Lord, at Christmas-
    tide,
Is there not peace upon earth, goodwill among men?
The peace of this world is always uncertain, unless men keep
    the peace of God.
And war among men defiles this world, but death in the
    Lord renews it,
And the world must be cleaned in the winter, or we shall
    have only
A sour spring, a parched summer, an empty harvest.
Between Christmas and Easter what work shall be done?
The ploughman shall go out in March and turn the same
    earth
He has turned before, the bird shall sing the same song.   20
When the leaf is out on the tree, when the elder and may
Burst over the stream, and the air is clear and high,

And voices trill at windows, and children tumble in front of
     the door,
What work shall have been done, what wrong
Shall the bird's song cover, the green tree cover, what wrong
Shall the fresh earth cover? We wait, and the time is short
But waiting is long.
[*Enter the* First Priest *with a banner of St. Stephen borne
     before him. The lines sung are in italics.*]

First Priest

Since Christmas a day: and the day of St. Stephen, First
     Martyr.
Princes moreover did sit, and did witness falsely against me.[1]
30 A day that was always most dear to the Archbishop
     Thomas.
And he knelt down and cried with a loud voice:
Lord, lay not this sin to their charge.
Princes moreover did sit.
                              [*Introit of St. Stephen is heard.*]
                    [*Enter the* Second Priest, *with a banner of St. John the
                              Apostle borne before him.*]

Second Priest

Since St. Stephen a day: and the day of St. John the Apostle.
In the midst of the congregation he opened his mouth.[2]
That which was from the beginning,[3] which we have heard,
Which we have seen with our eyes, and our hands have
     handled
Of the word of life; that which we have seen and heard
Declare we unto you.
40 *In the midst of the congregation.*
                              [*Introit of St. John is heard.*]
                    [*Enter the* Third Priest, *with a banner of the Holy
                              Innocents borne before him.*]

62

THIRD PRIEST

Since St. John the Apostle a day: and the day of the Holy
    Innocents.
Out of the mouth of very babes, O God.[4]
As the voice of many waters, of thunder, of harps,
They sung as it were a new song.[5]
The blood of thy saints[6] have they shed like water,
And there was no man to bury them.[7] Avenge, O Lord,
The blood of thy saints.[8] In Rama, a voice heard, weeping.[9]
Out of the mouth of very babes, O God!
(THE PRIESTS *stand together with the banners behind them.*]

FIRST PRIEST

Since the Holy Innocents a day: the fourth day from
    Christmas.

THE THREE PRIESTS

Rejoice we all, keeping holy day.[10]   50

FIRST PRIEST

As for the people, so also for himself, he offereth for sins.
He lays down his life for the sheep.[11]

THE THREE PRIESTS

Rejoice we all, keeping holy day.

FIRST PRIEST
                         To-day?

SECOND PRIEST

To-day, what is to-day?[12] For the day is half gone.

FIRST PRIEST

To-day, what is to-day? but another day, the dusk of the
    year.

SECOND PRIEST

To-day, what is to-day? Another night, and another dawn.

THIRD PRIEST

What day is the day that we know that we hope for or fear
    for?
Every day is the day we should fear from or hope from.
    One moment
Weighs like another. Only in retrospection, selection.
60 We say, that was the day. The critical moment
That is always now, and here. Even now, in sordid par-
    ticulars
The eternal design may appear.
[*Enter the* FOUR KNIGHTS. *The banners disappear.*]

FIRST KNIGHT

Servants of the King.[13]

FIRST PRIEST

         And known to us.
You are welcome. Have you ridden far?

FIRST KNIGHT

Not far to-day, but matters urgent
Have brought us from France. We rode hard,
Took ship yesterday, landed last night,
Having business with the Archbishop.

SECOND KNIGHT

Urgent business.

THIRD KNIGHT

From the King.

SECOND KNIGHT
By the King's order.   70

            FIRST KNIGHT
                    Our men are outside.

            FIRST PRIEST
You know the Archbishop's hospitality.
We are about to go to dinner.
The good Archbishop would be vexed
If we did not offer you entertainment
Before your business. Please dine with us.[14]
Your men shall be looked after also.
Dinner before business. Do you like roast pork?

            FIRST KNIGHT
Business before dinner. We will roast your pork
First, and dine upon it after.

            SECOND KNIGHT
We must see the Archbishop.   80

            THIRD KNIGHT
                        Go, tell the Archbishop
We have no need of his hospitality.
We will find our own dinner.

            FIRST PRIEST [*to attendant*]
Go, tell His Lordship.

            FOURTH KNIGHT
            How much longer will you keep us waiting?
[*Enter* THOMAS.]

            THOMAS [*to* PRIESTS]
However certain our expectation
                    65

The moment foreseen may be unexpected
When it arrives. It comes when we are
Engrossed with matters of other urgency.[15]
On my table you will find
The papers in order, and the documents signed.
[*To* KNIGHTS.]
90 You are welcome, whatever your business may be.
    You say, from the King?

FIRST KNIGHT
               Most surely from the King.
We must speak with you alone.

THOMAS [*to* PRIESTS]
                Leave us then alone.
Now what is the matter?

FIRST KNIGHT
           This is the matter.

THE THREE KNIGHTS
You are the Archbishop in revolt against the King; in
    rebellion to the King and the law of the land;
You are the Archbishop who was made by the King; whom
    he set in your place to carry out his command.
You are his servant, his tool, and his jack,
You wore his favours on your back,
You had your honours all from his hand; from him you had
    the power, the seal and the ring.
This is the man who was the tradesman's son: the back-
    stairs brat who was born in Cheapside;
100 This is the creature that crawled upon the King; swollen
    with blood and swollen with pride.
Creeping out of the London dirt,
Crawling up like a louse on your shirt,

The man who cheated, swindled, lied; broke his oath and
    betrayed his King.

THOMAS

This is not true.
Both before and after I received the ring
I have been a loyal subject to the King.
Saving my order,[16] I am at his command,
As his most faithful vassal in the land.

FIRST KNIGHT

Saving your order! let your order save you—
As I do not think it is like to do.   110
Saving your ambition is what you mean,
Saving your pride, envy and spleen.

SECOND KNIGHT

Saving your insolence and greed.
Won't you ask us to pray to God for you, in your need?

THIRD KNIGHT

Yes, we'll pray for you![17]

FIRST KNIGHT

        Yes, we'll pray for you!

THE THREE KNIGHTS

Yes, we'll pray that God may help you!

THOMAS

But, gentlemen, your business
Which you said so urgent, is it only
Scolding and blaspheming?

FIRST KNIGHT
                    That was only
120 Our indignation, as loyal subjects.

THOMAS
Loyal? to whom?

FIRST KNIGHT
To the King!

SECOND KNIGHT
                    The King!

THIRD KNIGHT
The King!

THE THREE KNIGHTS
God bless him!

THOMAS
Then let your new coat of loyalty be worn
Carefully, so it get not soiled or torn.
Have you something to say?

FIRST KNIGHT
                    By the King's command.
Shall we say it now?

SECOND KNIGHT
                    Without delay,
Before the old fox is off and away.

68

THOMAS

What you have to say
By the King's command—if it be the King's command—
Should be said in public. If you make charges,[18]
Then in public I will refute them.   130

FIRST KNIGHT

No! here and now!
[*They make to attack him, but the priests and attendants
return and quietly interpose themselves.*]

THOMAS

Now and here!

FIRST KNIGHT
Of your earlier misdeeds I shall make no mention.
They are too well known. But after dissension
Had ended, in France, and you were endued
With your former privilege, how did you show your grati-
      tude?
You had fled from England, not exiled
Or threatened, mind you; but in the hope
Of stirring up trouble in the French dominions.
You sowed strife abroad, you reviled
The King to the King of France, to the Pope,   140
Raising up against him false opinions.

SECOND KNIGHT
Yet the King, out of his charity,
And urged by your friends, offered clemency,
Made a pact of peace, and all dispute ended
Sent you back to your See as you demanded.

THIRD KNIGHT

And burying the memory of your transgressions
Restored your honours and your possessions.
All was granted for which you sued:
Yet how, I repeat, did you show your gratitude?

FIRST KNIGHT

150 Suspending those who had crowned the young prince,
Denying the legality of his coronation.

SECOND KNIGHT

Binding with the chains of anathema.

THIRD KNIGHT

Using every means in your power to evince[19]
The King's faithful servants, every one who transacts
His business in his absence, the business of the nation.

FIRST KNIGHT

These are the facts.
Say therefore if you will be content
To answer in the King's presence. Therefore were we sent.

THOMAS

Never was it my wish
160 To uncrown the King's son, or to diminish
His honour and power. Why should he wish
To deprive my people of me and keep me from my own
And bid me sit in Canterbury, alone?
I would wish him three crowns rather than one,
And as for the bishops,[20] it is not my yoke
That is laid upon them, or mine to revoke.
Let them go to the Pope. It was he who condemned them.

FIRST KNIGHT
Through you they were suspended.

SECOND KNIGHT
By you be this amended.

THIRD KNIGHT
Absolve them.

FIRST KNIGHT
Absolve them.

THOMAS
I do not deny
That this was done through me. But it is not I   170
Who can loose whom the Pope has bound.
Let them go to him, upon whom redounds
Their contempt towards me, their contempt towards the
Church shown.

FIRST KNIGHT
Be that as it may, here is the King's command:
That you and your servants depart from this land.

THOMAS
If that *is* the King's command, I will be bold
To say: seven years were my people without
My presence; seven years of misery and pain.
Seven years a mendicant on foreign charity
I lingered abroad: seven years is no brevity.   180
I shall not get those seven years back again.
Never again, you must make no doubt,
Shall the sea run between the shepherd and his fold.

FIRST KNIGHT

The King's justice, the King's majesty,
You insult with gross indignity;
Insolent madman, whom nothing deters
From attainting his servants and ministers.

THOMAS

It is not I who insult the King,
And there is higher than I or the King.
190 It is not I, Becket from Cheapside,
It is not against me, Becket, that you strive.
It is not Becket who pronounces doom,
But the Law of Christ's Church, the judgement of Rome.

FIRST KNIGHT

Priest, you have spoken in peril of your life.

SECOND KNIGHT

Priest, you have spoken in danger of the knife.

THIRD KNIGHT

Priest, you have spoken treachery and treason.

THE THREE KNIGHTS

Priest! traitor, confirmed in malfeasance.[21]

THOMAS

I submit my cause to the judgement of Rome.
But if you kill me, I shall rise from my tomb[22]
200 To submit my cause before God's throne.

[*Exit.*]

FOURTH KNIGHT
Priest! monk! and servant! take, hold, detain,
Restrain this man,[23] in the King's name.

FIRST KNIGHT
Or answer with your bodies.

SECOND KNIGHT
Enough of words.

THE FOUR KNIGHTS
We come for the King's justice, we come with swords.
[*Exeunt.*]

CHORUS
I have smelt them,[24] the death-bringers, senses are quickened
By subtile forebodings; I have heard
Fluting in the night-time, fluting and owls, have seen at noon
Scaly wings slanting over, huge and ridiculous. I have tasted
The savour of putrid flesh in the spoon. I have felt
The heaving of earth at nightfall, restless, absurd. I have 210 heard
Laughter in the noises of beasts that make strange noises: jackal, jackass, jackdaw; the scurrying noise of mouse and jerboa; the laugh of the loon, the lunatic bird. I have seen
Grey necks twisting, rat tails twining, in the thick light of dawn. I have eaten
Smooth creatures still living, with the strong salt taste of living things under sea; I have tasted
The living lobster, the crab, the oyster, the whelk and the prawn; and they live and spawn in my bowels, and my bowels dissolve in the light of dawn. I have smelt

Death in the rose, death in the hollyhock, sweet pea,
    hyacinth, primrose and cowslip, I have seen
Trunk and horn, tusk and hoof, in odd places;
I have lain on the floor of the sea and breathed with the
    breathing of the sea-anemone, swallowed with ingur-
    gitation of the sponge. I have lain in the soil and criti-
    cised the worm. In the air
Flirted with the passage of the kite. I have plunged with
    the kite and cowered with the wren. I have felt
The horn of the beetle, the scale of the viper, the mobile
    hard insensitive skin of the elephant, the evasive flank
    of the fish. I have smelt
220 Corruption in the dish, incense in the latrine, the sewer in
    the incense, the smell of sweet soap in the woodpath, a
    hellish sweet scent in the woodpath, while the ground
    heaved. I have seen
Rings of light coiling downwards, descending
To the horror of the ape. Have I not known, not known
What was coming to be? It was here, in the kitchen, in the
    passage,
In the mews in the barn in the byre in the market-place
In our veins our bowels our skulls as well
As well as in the plottings of potentates
As well as in the consultations of powers.
What is woven on the loom of fate
What is woven in the councils of princes
230 Is woven also in our veins, our brains,
Is woven like a pattern of living worms
In the guts of the women of Canterbury.

I have smelt them, the death-bringers; now is too late
For action, too soon for contrition.
Nothing is possible but the shamed swoon
Of those consenting to the last humiliation.

I have consented, Lord Archbishop, have consented.[25]
Am torn away,[26] subdued, violated,
United to the spiritual flesh of nature,
Mastered by the animal powers of spirit,   240
Dominated by the lust of self-demolition,
By the final utter uttermost death of spirit,
By the final ecstasy of waste and shame,[27]
O Lord Archbishop, O Thomas Archbishop, forgive us, for-
    give us, pray for us that we may pray for you, out of
    our shame.
[*Enter* THOMAS.]

THOMAS

Peace, and be at peace with your thoughts and visions.
These things had to come to you and you accept them,
This is your share of the eternal burden,
The perpetual glory.[28] This is one moment,
But know that another
Shall pierce you with a sudden painful joy   250
When the figure of God's purpose is made complete.
You shall forget these things, toiling in the household,
You shall remember them, droning by the fire,
When age and forgetfulness sweeten memory
Only like a dream that has often been told
And often been changed in the telling. They will seem
    unreal.
Human kind cannot bear very much reality.
[*Enter* PRIESTS.]

PRIESTS [*severally*]

My Lord, you must not stop here.[29] To the minster.
Through the cloister. No time to waste. They are
coming back, armed. To the altar, to the altar.

THOMAS

All my life they have been coming, these feet. All my life
260 I have waited. Death will come only when I am worthy,
And if I am worthy, there is no danger.
I have therefore only to make perfect my will.[30]

PRIESTS

My Lord, they are coming. They will break through
     presently.
You will be killed. Come to the altar.
Make haste, my Lord. Don't stop here talking. It is not
     right.
What shall become of us, my Lord, if you are killed; what
     shall become of us?

THOMAS

Peace! be quiet! remember where you are, and what is
     happening;
No life here is sought for but mine,
And I am not in danger: only near to death.

PRIESTS

270 My Lord, to vespers! You must not be absent from vespers.
     You must not be absent from the divine office. To
     vespers. Into the cathedral!

THOMAS

Go to vespers, remember me at your prayers.
They shall find the shepherd here; the flock shall be spared.
I have had a tremor of bliss, a wink of heaven, a whisper,
And I would no longer be denied; all things
Proceed to a joyful consummation.

PRIESTS

Seize him! force him! drag him!

THOMAS

Keep your hands off!

PRIESTS

To vespers! Hurry.
[*They drag him off. While the* CHORUS *speak, the scene is
changed to the cathedral.*]
CHORUS [*while a* Dies Iræ[31] *is sung in Latin by a choir in the
distance.*]
Numb the hand and dry the eyelid,
Still the horror, but more horror   280
Than when tearing in the belly.

Still the horror, but more horror
Than when twisting in the fingers,
Than when splitting in the skull.

More than footfall in the passage,
More than shadow in the doorway,
More than fury in the hall.

The agents of hell disappear, the human, they shrink and
      dissolve
Into dust on the wind, forgotten, unmemorable; only is here
The white flat face of Death, God's silent servant,   290
And behind the face of Death the Judgement

And behind the Judgement the Void,[32] more horrid than
      active shapes of hell;
Emptiness, absence, separation from God;
The horror of the effortless journey, to the empty land
Which is no land, only emptiness, absence, the Void,
Where those who were men can no longer turn the mind
To distraction, delusion, escape into dream, pretence,

Where the soul is no longer deceived, for there are no
    objects, no tones,
No colours, no forms to distract, to divert the soul
300 From seeing itself, foully united forever, nothing with
    nothing,
Not what we call death, but what beyond death is not death,
We fear, we fear. Who shall then plead for me,
Who intercede for me, in my most need?[33]

Dead upon the tree, my Saviour,
Let not be in vain Thy labour;
Help me, Lord, in my last fear.

Dust I am, to dust am bending,
From the final doom impending
Help me, Lord, for death is near.

[*In the cathedral.* THOMAS *and* PRIESTS.]

PRIESTS

310 Bar the door.[34] Bar the door.
The door is barred.
We are safe. We are safe.
They dare not break in.
They cannot break in. They have not the force.
We are safe. We are safe.

THOMAS

Unbar the doors! throw open the doors!
I will not have the house of prayer, the church of Christ,
The sanctuary, turned into a fortress.[35]
The Church shall protect her own, in her own way, not
320 As oak and stone; stone and oak decay,
Give no stay, but the Church shall endure.

The church shall be open, even to our enemies. Open the
    door!

First Priest

My Lord! these are not men, these come not as men come,
    but
Like maddened beasts. They come not like men, who
Respect the sanctuary, who kneel to the Body of Christ,
But like beasts. You would bar the door
Against the lion, the leopard, the wolf or the boar,
Why not more
Against beasts with the souls of damned men, against men
Who would damn themselves to beasts. My Lord! My Lord! 330

Thomas

Unbar the door!
You think me reckless, desperate and mad.
You argue by results, as this world does,
To settle if an act be good or bad.
You defer to the fact. For every life and every act
Consequence of good and evil can be shown.
And as in time results of many deeds are blended
So good and evil in the end become confounded.
It is not in time that my death shall be known;[36]
It is out of time that my decision is taken   340
If you call that decision
To which my whole being gives entire consent.
I give my life
To the Law of God above the Law of Man.
Unbar the door! unbar the door!
We are not here to triumph by fighting, by stratagem, or
    by resistance,
Not to fight with beasts as men. We have fought the beast
And have conquered. We have only to conquer
Now, by suffering. This is the easier victory.

350 Now is the triumph of the Cross, now
Open the door! I command it. OPEN THE DOOR!
[*The door is opened. The* KNIGHTS *enter, slightly tipsy.*]

PRIESTS

This way, my Lord! Quick. Up the stair. To the roof. To
the crypt. Quick. Come. Force him.

KNIGHTS

Where is Becket, the traitor to the King?
Where is Becket, the meddling priest?
Come down Daniel to the lions' den,[37]
Come down Daniel for the mark of the beast.[38]

Are you washed in the blood of the Lamb?
Are you marked with the mark of the beast?
Come down Daniel to the lions' den,
360   Come down Daniel and join in the feast.

Where is Becket the Cheapside brat?
Where is Becket the faithless priest?
Come down Daniel to the lions' den,
Come down Daniel and join in the feast.

THOMAS

It is the just man who
Like a bold lion, should be without fear.
I am here.
No traitor to the King. I am a priest,
A Christian, saved by the blood of Christ,
370 Ready to suffer with my blood.
This is the sign of the Church always,
The sign of blood. Blood for blood.
His blood given to buy my life,

My blood given to pay for his death,
My death for His death.

FIRST KNIGHT

Absolve all those you have excommunicated.

SECOND KNIGHT

Resign the powers you have arrogated.

THIRD KNIGHT

Restore to the King the money you appropriated.

FIRST KNIGHT

Renew the obedience you have violated.

THOMAS

For my Lord I am now ready to die,   380
That his Church may have peace and liberty.
Do with me as you will,[39] to your hurt and shame;
But none of my people, in God's name,
Whether layman or clerk, shall you touch.
This I forbid.

KNIGHTS

Traitor! traitor! traitor!

THOMAS

You, Reginald, three times traitor you:
Traitor to me as my temporal vassal,[40]
Traitor to me as your spiritual lord,
Traitor to God in desecrating His Church.   390

FIRST KNIGHT

No faith do I owe to a renegade,
And what I owe shall now be paid.

THOMAS

Now to Almighty God,[41] to the Blessed Mary ever Virgin,
to the blessed John the Baptist, the holy apostles Peter and
Paul, to the blessed martyr Denys, and to all the Saints, I
commend my cause and that of the Church.

While the KNIGHTS *kill him,*[42] *we hear the*
CHORUS

Clear the air![43] clean the sky! wash the wind! take stone
    from stone and wash them.
The land is foul, the water is foul, our beasts and ourselves
    defiled with blood.
A rain of blood has blinded my eyes. Where is England?
    where is Kent? where is Canterbury?
400 O far far far far in the past; and I wander in a land of barren
    boughs: if I break them, they bleed; I wander in a
    land of dry stones: if I touch them they bleed.
How how can I ever return, to the soft quiet seasons?
Night stay with us, stop sun, hold season, let the day not
    come, let the spring not come.
Can I look again at the day and its common things, and see
    them all smeared with blood, through a curtain of
    falling blood?
We did not wish anything to happen.
We understood the private catastrophe,
The personal loss, the general misery,
Living and partly living;
The terror by night that ends in daily action,
The terror by day that ends in sleep;
410 But the talk in the market-place, the hand on the broom,

The night-time heaping of the ashes,
The fuel laid on the fire at daybreak,
These acts marked a limit to our suffering.
Every horror had its definition,
Every sorrow had a kind of end:
In life there is not time to grieve long.
But this, this is out of life, this is out of time,
An instant eternity of evil and wrong.
We are soiled by a filth that we cannot clean, united to
    supernatural vermin,
It is not we alone, it is not the house, it is not the city that is 420
    defiled,
But the world that is wholly foul.
Clear the air! clean the sky! wash the wind! take the stone
    from the stone, take the skin from the arm, take the
    muscle from the bone, and wash them. Wash the stone,
    wash the bone, wash the brain, wash the soul, wash
    them wash them!

[*The* KNIGHTS, *having completed the murder, advance to
the front of the stage and address the audience.*][44]

FIRST KNIGHT

We beg you to give us your attention for a few moments.
We know that you may be disposed to judge unfavourably
of our action. You are Englishmen, and therefore you believe in fair play: and when you see one man being set upon
by four, then your sympathies are all with the under dog. I
respect such feelings, I share them. Nevertheless, I appeal
to your sense of honour. You are Englishmen, and therefore
will not judge anybody without hearing both sides of the 430
case. That is in accordance with our long-established principle of Trial by Jury. I am not myself qualified to put our
case to you. I am a man of action and not of words. For that
reason I shall do no more than introduce the other speakers,

who, with their various abilities, and different points of
view, will be able to lay before you the merits of this extremely complex problem. I shall call upon our eldest
member to speak first, my neighbour in the country:
Baron William de Traci.

Third Knight

440   I am afraid I am not anything like such an experienced
speaker as my old friend Reginald Fitz Urse would lead you
to believe. But there is one thing I should like to say, and I
might as well say it at once. It is this: in what we have done,
and whatever you may think of it, we have been perfectly
disinterested. [*The other* KNIGHTS: 'Hear! hear!'.] *We* are
not getting anything out of this. We have much more to lose
than to gain. We are four plain Englishmen who put our
country first. I dare say that we didn't make a very good
impression when we came in just now. The fact is that we
450 knew we had taken on a pretty stiff job; I'll only speak for
myself, but I had drunk a good deal—I am not a drinking
man ordinarily—to brace myself up for it. When you
come to the point, it does go against the grain to kill an
Archbishop, especially when you have been brought up in
good Church traditions. So if we seemed a bit rowdy, you
will understand why it was; and for my part I am awfully
sorry about it. We realised this was our duty, but all the
same we had to work ourselves up to it. And, as I said, *we*
are not getting a penny out of this. We know perfectly well
460 how things will turn out. King Henry—God bless him—
will have to say, for reasons of state, that he never meant
this to happen; and there is going to be an awful row; and
at the best we shall have to spend the rest of our lives abroad.
And even when reasonable people come to see that the
Archbishop *had* to be put out of the way—and personally
I had a tremendous admiration for him—you must have

noticed what a good show he put up at the end—they won't give *us* any glory. No, we have done for ourselves, there's no mistake about that. So, as I said at the beginning, please give us at least the credit for being completely dis- 470
interested in this business. I think that is about all I have to say.

FIRST KNIGHT

I think we will all agree that William de Traci has spoken well and has made a very important point. The gist of his argument is this: that we have been completely disinter-ested. But our act itself needs more justification than that; and you must hear our other speakers. I shall next call upon Hugh de Morville, who has made a special study of state-craft and constitutional law. Sir Hugh de Morville.

SECOND KNIGHT

I should like first to recur to a point that was very well 480
put by our leader, Reginald Fitz Urse: that you are Eng-lishmen, and therefore your sympathies are always with the under dog. It is the English spirit of fair play. Now the worthy Archbishop, whose good qualities I very much ad-mired, has throughout been presented as the under dog. But is this really the case? I am going to appeal not to your emotions but to your reason. You are hard-headed sensible people, as I can see, and not to be taken in by emotional claptrap. I therefore ask you to consider soberly: what were the Archbishop's aims? and what are King Henry's aims? 490
In the answer to these questions lies the key to the problem.

The King's aim has been perfectly consistent. During the reign of the late Queen Matilda and the irruption of the un-happy usurper Stephen, the kingdom was very much divided. Our King saw the one thing needful was to restore order: to curb the excessive powers of local government, which were usually exercised for selfish and often for seditious ends, and to reform the legal system. He therefore intended that Becket, who had proved himself an extremely 500 able administrator—no one denies that—should unite the offices of Chancellor and Archbishop. Had Becket concurred with the King's wishes, we should have had an almost ideal State: a union of spiritual and temporal administration, under the central government. I knew Becket well, in various official relations; and I may say that I have never known a man so well qualified for the highest rank of the Civil Service. And what happened? The moment that Becket, at the King's instance, had been made Archbishop, he resigned the office of Chancellor, he became more priestly 510 than the priests, he ostentatiously and offensively adopted an ascetic manner of life, he affirmed immediately that there was a higher order than that which our King, and he as the King's servant, had for so many years striven to establish; and that—God knows why—the two orders were incompatible.

You will agree with me that such interference by an Archbishop offends the instincts of a people like ours. So far, I know that I have your approval: I read it in your faces. It is only with the measures we have had to adopt, in order to 520 set matters to rights, that you take issue. No one regrets the necessity for violence more than we do. Unhappily, there are times when violence is the only way in which social justice can be secured. At another time, you would condemn an Archbishop by vote of Parliament and execute him formally as a traitor, and no one would have to bear the burden of being called murderer. And at a later time still, even such temperate measures as these would become unnecessary. But, if you have now arrived at a just subordination of the pretensions of the Church to the welfare of the State, re- 530 member that it is we who took the first step. We have been instrumental in bringing about the state of affairs that you approve. We have served your interests; we merit your applause; and if there is any guilt whatever in the matter, you must share it with us.

FIRST KNIGHT

Morville has given us a great deal to think about. It seems to me that he has said almost the last word, for those who have been able to follow his very subtle reasoning. We have, however, one more speaker, who has I think another point of view to express. If there are any who are still un- convinced, I think that Richard Brito, coming as he does of 540 a family distinguished for its loyalty to the Church, will be able to convince them. Richard Brito.

FOURTH KNIGHT

The speakers who have preceded me, to say nothing of our leader, Reginald Fitz Urse, have all spoken very much to the point. I have nothing to add along their particular lines of argument. What I have to say may be put in the form of a question: *Who killed the Archbishop?* As you have been eyewitnesses of this lamentable scene, you may feel some surprise at my putting it in this way. But consider the course of events. I am obliged, very briefly, to go over the 550 ground traversed by the last speaker. While the late Arch- bishop was Chancellor, no one, under the King, did more to weld the country together, to give it the unity, the stability, order, tranquillity, and justice that it so badly needed. From the moment he became Archbishop, he completely reversed his policy; he showed himself to be utterly indif- ferent to the fate of the country, to be, in fact, a monster of egotism. This egotism grew upon him, until it became at last an undoubted mania. I have unimpeachable evidence to the effect that before he left France he clearly prophesied, 560 in the presence of numerous witnesses, that he had not long

to live, and that he would be killed in England. He used
every means of provocation; from his conduct, step by
step, there can be no inference except that he had determined upon a death by martyrdom. Even at the last, he
could have given us reason: you have seen how he evaded
our questions. And when he had deliberately exasperated
us beyond human endurance, he could still have easily
escaped; he could have kept himself from us long enough to
570 allow our righteous anger to cool. That was just what he
did not wish to happen; he insisted, while we were still in-
flamed with wrath, that the doors should be opened. Need
I say more? I think, with these facts before you, you will
unhesitatingly render a verdict of Suicide while of Unsound Mind. It is the only charitable verdict you can give,
upon one who was, after all, a great man.

First Knight

Thank you, Brito, I think that there is no more to be said;
and I suggest that you now disperse quietly to your homes.
Please be careful not to loiter in groups at street corners,
580 and do nothing that might provoke any public outbreak.
[*Exeunt* Knights.]

First Priest

O father, father, gone from us, lost to us,
How shall we find you, from what far place
Do you look down on us? You now in Heaven,
Who shall now guide us, protect us, direct us?
After what journey through what further dread
Shall we recover your presence? when inherit
Your strength? The Church lies bereft,
Alone, desecrated, desolated, and the heathen shall build
      on the ruins,
Their world without God.[45] I see it. I see it.

THIRD PRIEST

No. For the Church is stronger for this action,   590
Triumphant in adversity. It is fortified
By persecution: supreme, so long as men will die for it.
Go, weak sad men, lost erring souls, homeless in earth or
    heaven.
Go where the sunset reddens the last grey rock
Of Brittany, or the Gates of Hercules.
Go venture shipwreck on the sullen coasts
Where blackamoors make captive Christian men;
Go to the northern seas confined with ice
Where the dead breath makes numb the hand, makes dull
    the brain;
Find an oasis in the desert sun,   600
Go seek alliance with the heathen Saracen,
To share his filthy rites,[46] and try to snatch
Forgetfulness in his libidinous courts,
Oblivion in the fountain by the date-tree;
Or sit and bite your nails in Aquitaine.
In the small circle of pain within the skull
You still shall tramp and tread one endless round
Of thought, to justify your action to yourselves,
Weaving a fiction which unravels as you weave,
Pacing forever in the hell of make-believe[47]   610
Which never is belief: this is your fate on earth
And we must think no further of you.

FIRST PRIEST
                O my lord
The glory of whose new state is hidden from us,
Pray for us of your charity.

SECOND PRIEST
              Now in the sight of God

Conjoined with all the saints and martyrs gone before you,
Remember us.

THIRD PRIEST
Let our thanks ascend
To God, who has given us another Saint in Canterbury.

CHORUS. [*While a* Te Deum *is sung in Latin by a choir in
the distance.*]
We praise Thee, O God, for Thy glory displayed in all the
    creatures of the earth,
In the snow, in the rain, in the wind, in the storm; in all of
    Thy creatures, both the hunters and the hunted.
620 For all things exist only as seen by Thee, only as known by
    Thee, all things exist
Only in Thy light, and Thy glory is declared even in that
    which denies Thee; the darkness declares the glory of
    light.
Those who deny Thee could not deny, if Thou didst not
    exist; and their denial is never complete, for if it were
    so, they would not exist.
They affirm Thee in living; all things affirm Thee in living;
    the bird in the air, both the hawk and the finch; the
    beast on the earth, both the wolf and the lamb; the
    worm in the soil and the worm in the belly.
Therefore man, whom Thou hast made to be conscious of
    Thee, must consciously praise Thee, in thought and in
    word and in deed.
Even with the hand to the broom, the back bent in laying
    the fire, the knee bent in cleaning the hearth, we, the
    scrubbers and sweepers of Canterbury,
The back bent under toil, the knee bent under sin, the hands
    to the face under fear, the head bent under grief,

Even in us the voices of seasons, the snuffle of winter, the
    song of spring, the drone of summer, the voices of
    beasts and of birds, praise Thee.
We thank Thee for Thy mercies of blood, for Thy redemp-
    tion by blood. For the blood of Thy martyrs and saints
Shall enrich the earth, shall create the holy places.
For wherever a saint has dwelt, wherever a martyr has 630
    given his blood for the blood of Christ,
There is holy ground, and the sanctity shall not depart
    from it
Though armies trample over it, though sightseers come
    with guide-books looking over it;
From where the western seas gnaw at the coast of Iona,
To the death in the desert, the prayer in forgotten places
    by the broken imperial column,
From such ground springs that which forever renews the
    earth
Though it is forever denied. Therefore, O God, we thank
    Thee
Who hast given such blessing to Canterbury.

Forgive us, O Lord, we acknowledge ourselves as type of
    the common man,
 Of the men and women who shut the door and sit by the fire;
Who fear the blessing of God, the loneliness of the night of 640
    God,[48] the surrender required, the deprivation
    inflicted;
Who fear the injustice of men less than the justice of God;
Who fear the hand at the window, the fire in the thatch, the
    fist in the tavern, the push into the canal,
Less than we fear the love of God.
We acknowledge our trespass, our weakness, our fault; we
    acknowledge
That the sin of the world is upon our heads; that the blood

of the martyrs and the agony of the saints
Is upon our heads.
Lord, have mercy upon us.
Christ, have mercy upon us.
Lord, have mercy upon us.
650 Blessed Thomas, pray for us.

Notes

NOTES

*Frequent reference will be made in these notes to the collection
of contemporary source-material describing the life and death
of Thomas Becket and the events consequent upon it. This
collection is entitled* Materials for the History of Thomas
Becket, Archbishop of Canterbury, *and was edited for the
Rolls Series by James Craigie Robertson in seven volumes
published in 1875. I shall refer to this work as* Materials,
adding the appropriate volume, page and author.

INTRODUCTION

1. *The Assassins.* These four men, remembered only for
the terrible moment of their crime, about which every
detail is known, have no other history. They were all
what may loosely be called 'barons', men who held land
directly from the Crown and were part of the King's
entourage, on the occasion of his visit to Bures near
Bayeux in December 1170. Reginald Fitz Urse, who
seems to have been their self-constituted leader, held
land in Kent, Somerset and Northampton; he seems
also to have been in some kind of feudal relationship
with Becket, for when he tried to lay hands on him the
Archbishop said '*Recede hinc ; homo meus es, contingere
me non debes!*' ('Get out of this; you are my man. You
have no business to touch me') (*Materials*, IV, p. 76,
Anonymous Author I). De Traci came from a family
that held land in Devonshire and Gloucestershire; he
too was a dependant of Becket's. Hugh de Morville's
father held land in Cumberland and Hugh owned a

castle at Knaresborough in Yorkshire; he was a witness to the Constitutions of Clarendon. I do not know where Richard Brito came from.

The King had tried to arrange for the peaceful succession of his son to the throne by having him crowned in advance, and as he was at loggerheads with the Archbishop of Canterbury over the Constitutions of Clarendon, he had induced the Archbishop of York, assisted by the Bishops of London and Salisbury, to carry out this coronation. But to crown the King of England had always been the unquestioned prerogative of the Archbishop of Canterbury, and Becket instantly took action against this infringement of the rights of his See by suspending the prelates in question and inducing the Pope to confirm their suspension. News of this reached King Henry at Bayeux; he was a man of great violence of temper and on this occasion he probably said more than he meant; but it was enough for Fitz Urse to gather de Traci, de Morville and Brito round him and together they decided to cross to England, and demand the cancellation of the Archbishop's action against his subordinate bishops, at the sword's point. They crossed the Channel by different routes and joined up at Saltwood Castle, then held by Ranulf de Broc, a man of similar feudal status and opinions.

It is probable that these men were wicked by stupidity; they had got it into their feudal heads that since Becket had been appointed to the Archbishopric by the King, he was the King's 'man', and his appeal to the Pope, over the King's head, was therefore treason. Treason is a powerful and heady word and a stupid man can easily inebriate himself with it, so that he appears to himself in a heroic light; it would seem from the *Materials* that the Four Knights did not intend murder at first, for when they came to demand an interview with the Archbishop, they came unarmed. They were civilly received and invited to a meal, which they refused. They asked to see Becket alone and he dismissed his attendants; but when they stated their business (which was to demand the reinstatement of the peccant Archbishop of York and his confederates) he recalled his monks, for he said that a message of this kind was of a public character, to be heard by all.

He gave answer that the matter was out of his hands, since the Pope had taken action; he therefore no longer had power to cancel their suspension. The Knights then clattered off to arm themselves and returned presently to accomplish their mission by murder. The murder took place very much in the manner in which it is presented in the play, but more brutally. Eliot, more concerned with its inward meaning than with its sensational fury, has softened it into a symbol of his thoughts on the interrelationship between acts in Time and acts in Eternity.

After the murder the Knights returned in triumph to Saltwood, having looted the archiepiscopal palace on the way. Christendom was astounded by the abomination they had committed and the Pope excommunicated them the instant the news reached Rome. By the King's advice the Knights fled to Scotland, and from this point onward their history begins to turn into legend. It is said that in Scotland the people were for hanging them out of hand; so they twisted back to Knaresborough and took refuge in de Morville's castle. There the very dogs refused to eat with them. The King advised their submission to the Pope, and they seem indeed to have presented themselves before him as penitents in Rome; he gave them the maximum penance in his power—a perpetual fast and a pilgrimage to Jerusalem. What happened after is uncertain; by one account they reached Jerusalem and died there; by another, de Traci got to Cosenza in Sicily, where he died of a shocking disease that caused the flesh to rot off his bones while he was still alive; he never ceased (says the story) praying to St. Thomas, whom he had helped to murder, for his intercession. Some say Fitz Urse returned from Jerusalem and went to Ireland, where he founded a family. There is record of a Hugh de Morville who had the right to hold a manorial court in 1200, but it may not be the same man. These four men only exist for posterity because of the moment of their murder and of that there are accounts as detailed and as corroborative, on the whole, as you would find in any dozen newspapers on the morning after an important assassination to-day, such, for instance, as that of President Kennedy. But all the accounts of Becket's murder come from his supporters and partisans and it is hard, as Samuel Butler has remarked to judge between God and the Devil, 'for God has written all the books'.

2. *Agonotheta Dei. Agonotheta* is a term for the Master of Ceremonies in an athletic contest during classical times, and is used of St. Thomas by one of his monks, William of Canterbury, to mean 'Chief Contestor for God' (*Materials*, I, p. 132).

3. *Athleta Christi.* As we should say, 'Christ's Prize-Fighter', a phrase describing St. Thomas in a letter from Herbert of Bosham, his friend and secretary, to Pope Alexander (*Materials*, VII, p. 430).

4. *Materials*, II, p. 437, account of Edward Grim: '*Nefandus miles . . . insiliit in eum subito, et summitate coronae, quam sancti chrismatis unctio dicaverat Deo,*

abrasa, agnum Deo immolandum vulneravit in capite, eodem ictu praeciso brachio haec referentis.' ('The unspeakable knight leapt suddenly upon him, and wounded the lamb to be sacrificed to God in the head, having cut into the top of that crown which the anointing of holy consecration had dedicated to God; by the same blow the arm of him who tells these things being cut through.')

5. F. M. Cornford, *The Origin of Attic Comedy*, first published 1914.
6. See Appendix III on Tennyson's *Becket*.
7. See Appendix II on *The Verse of Everyman*.
8. From *The Ascent of Mt. Carmel*, by St. John of the Cross.
9. Samuel Johnson, *Preface to the Dictionary*.
10. Christ said 'Be ye therefore perfect' (Matthew, v. 48).
11. T. S. Eliot, *Poetry and Drama*, 1951, p. 26.
12. For instance in the earliest known liturgical drama performed in England, in the middle of the tenth century, called the *Quem Quaeritis*, in which the three Marys, seeking the entombed Christ, find his sepulchre empty; an angel appears to them and tells them of his resurrection, and bids them announce it to the disciples. They turn towards the choir and give their message; and the choir and congregation break into *Te Deum Laudamus*. So too at the end of *The Castle of Perseverance*, a play belonging to the first quarter of the fifteenth century, the soul of the chief character, *Humanum Genus*, is saved through the merits of Christ, and the whole cast breaks out into a *Te Deum*.

THE TEXT. PART I

1. (line 2) *Are we drawn by danger?* The choric function of setting a mood of fear and doom is achieved by what

seems the natural reaction of poor women expecting more trouble; they seem dimly aware of some rumour of the Archbishop's return (line 21 and have an intuition that all will not be well if he does come, however much they need his presence. It is natural for them to crowd together for comfort, and seek the cathedral for sanctuary, perhaps for prayer, while knowing that even a cathedral can be desecrated; but they also realise that in any case such folk as they are need fear nothing for themselves, since nobody bothers about them; they are too unimportant. It is the more touching that Thomas bothers about them later in the play, taking them into his confidence in a sermon specially preached for them.

2. (line 8) *We are forced to bear witness*. The Greek word μάρτυρ means *witness*, and the women of Canterbury are to witness a martyrdom, in which they share, in so far as they witness it and suffer. They too are to be a kind of martyr.

3. (line 9) *Since golden October, etc*. The imagery from the seasons, repeated towards the end of this chorus, insists upon the endless cycle of Time and the returning years in which we live lives that are meaningless without relation to some eternal purpose outside Time. Compare the imagery of sidereal time which opens *The Rock* and of the seasons that opens *The Family Reunion*. The first dramatic treatment of this idea comes in the second fragment of *Sweeney Agonistes*, where Sweeney pictures the endless succession of morning, evening, noontide, night, birth, copulation and death, on a cannibal isle.

4. (lines 14–16) *Who has stretched out his hand to the fire, etc*. The Chorus are reminding themselves of the Feast of St. Michael and All Angels (All Hallows) a month or

so before (September 29). Did they and their fellow-cottagers of Canterbury really remember the saints and martyrs, as they stretched out their hands to the fire? Did not St. Peter stretch out his hand to the fire also, when he denied his Master (Mark, xiv. 66–8)? Implied in these questions are the further questions: will not another saint, their Archbishop, soon be among them? Will they behave like St. Peter and deny their master too?

5. (line 18) *Seven years, etc.* i.e. 1164–1170.

6. (line 31) *Winter shall come bringing death from the sea.* The Chorus has prophetic intuition, vaguely apprehended, of the crossing of the sea by the Four Knights, who came over from France to do their work (*Materials*, IV, p. 128, Anonymous Author II). The Chorus affirms this intuition metaphorically saying (line 43) 'I have seen these things in a shaft of sunlight'. In the first speech made by Thomas after his entry he says 'They speak better than they know' (line 207).

7. (line 47) *Happy December.* Happy because it is the month of the birth of Christ, and (though they do not know it) because of the martyrdom of Thomas, about to happen.

8. (line 60) *Frequent malversation.* The frequent misappropriation of money, designed for one purpose and wrongfully spent upon another.

9. (line 88) *Scenes of frenzied enthusiasm. Materials*, III, pp. 478–9, bear this out.

10. (line 92) *His horse will be deprived of his tail.* This comic notion, that reminds one of Antony's speech over the body of Caesar in Shakespeare's *Julius Caesar* ('Yea, beg a hair of him for memory', etc.) seems actually to have been suggested by a nasty anecdote recorded by Herbert of Bosham (*Materials*, III, p. 483) about

101

Robert de Broc, related to the Broc who had received the murderer-Knights into his castle at Saltwood; Herbert says that to show his contempt of the Archbishop he mutilated a horse of his by docking its tail.

11. (line 97) *But not the kiss of peace.* An attempt at a reconciliation between King Henry and Thomas was made on St. Mary Magdalen's Day (22 July) 1170, but it was little better than an uneasy truce. Thomas demanded the formal kiss of peace, but Henry refused it (*Materials*, III, p. 111, William Fitzstephen).

12. (line 106) *My Lord, he said, I leave you as a man, etc.* *Materials*, III, p. 116, William Fitzstephen: '*Domine, dicit mihi animus quod sic descedo a vobis quasi quem amplius in hac vita non videbitis.*' ('My lord, my soul tells me that I leave your presence as one whom in this life you will not see again.')

13. (line 121) *By temporal devolution.* i.e. devolving, or descending upon him from a temporal (not eternal) authority, namely that of a secular king, a source of this world's power.

14. (line 136) *I am the Archbishop's man.* This shows the same overrulingly feudal point of view among the clergy that they shared with their enemies, the Four Knights. No principle is safe from the stupidity of its supporters. Eliot is careful to show the superiority of the leader to the led in the case of Thomas and his monks.

15. (line 141) *Until the grinders cease, etc.* An allusion to the famous passage in the last chapter of Ecclesiastes, that seems to foretell the end of all things: 'In the day when the keepers of the house shall tremble, and the strong men shall bow themselves, *and the grinders cease because they are few*, and those that look out of the windows be darkened, *and the doors shall be shut in the*

streets, when the sound of the grinding is low, and he shall rise up at the voice of the bird, *and all the daughters of music shall be brought 'low'* (Ecclesiastes, XII. 3–4).

16. (line 144) *Here is no continuing city.* 'For here we have no continuing city' (Hebrews, XIII. 14).

17. (line 150) *You come bringing death into Canterbury.* The visionary fears of the Chorus grow with the scene and take more certain shape in their minds.

18. (line 155) *Living and partly living.* This phrase, used in this chorus and later as a refrain, has significance on two planes, the worldly plane, on which the poverty of these women prevents them from living much above subsistence level, and the spiritual plane, on which, having been seven years leaderless, they have lost courage, and their best hope is to succeed in 'avoiding notice', while they carry on village routine, and keep the feasts and masses of the church, much as they brew beer and cider, and undertake other necessary chores. Later in the speech (line 190) they beg to be left out of the oncoming doom of which their premonitions warn them, repeating that they are 'small folk' and begging Thomas to return to France—not at all on his account, but on their own. They are a spiritless lot; but as the play goes on they regain some spiritual stature, under the guidance of Thomas. I do not know of any other dramatic Chorus which *changes its moral character* during the course of a play. Eliot has treated this classic device in a revolutionary, naturalistic way. For instance, in the passage under discussion they show themselves in a cowardly cringe; compare the genuine humility of the last chorus of all (Part II, line 638 onwards).

19. (line 192) *Unaffrayed*, a word coined by Eliot, perhaps from an earlier *affrayed*, used by Keats in *The Eve of*

St. Agnes, xxxiii, where it appears to mean *startled*.
Keats was no doubt seeking an archaic effect by reminding us of *affray* from which our *afraid* derives. Eliot, in
using a like spelling (which appeals of course only to the
reader, not to a theatre-audience) is contrasting the fear
of the Chorus-women, whose brains are 'unskinned like
the layers of an onion' (compare *frayed*) with the imper-
turbability of Thomas, whose fate they believe to be
secure. They know, and they do not know, what the
audience already knows, that there will be an *affray* in
which Thomas will be martyred, and will yet be 'secure'
in sanctity. I think this play of irony is intended in
Eliot's deliberate, but archaic spelling. *Among the
shades* seems to refer forward to the *shadows* (252), that
is, to the Tempters.

20. (line 208) *They know and do not know*. See the Introduction, pages 17–18.

21. (line 234) *Rebellious bishops*. The Archbishop of York
and the Bishops of London and Salisbury had officiated
at the coronation of the young Henry, in defiance of
the fact that this was the prerogative of the See of
Canterbury (*Materials*, III, p. 458).

22. (line 241) *Broc, Warenne, and the Sheriff of Kent*.
Ranulf de Broc, a close associate of the Four Knights,
at whose castle at Saltwood they stayed the nights
before and after the murder. He was an old enemy of
Becket's (*Materials*, I, p. 100, William of Canterbury).
He and Gervase de Cornehill, Sheriff of Kent, together
with Reginald de Warenne, brother of the Earl of
Salisbury, are described by William of Canterbury as
the head of a gang that tried to oppose the return of
Becket at the port of Sandwich.

23. (line 243) *John, the Dean of Salisbury*. John of Oxford,
Dean of Salisbury, withstood Broc, Warenne and

Gervase and warning them of the dangers of treason, persuaded them to a conference with the Archbishop which resulted in his unmolested return to Canterbury (*ibid.*).

24. (line 255 onwards) *The Tempters*. Several things here call for note.

(A) There is no stage direction ordering the exit of Priests and Chorus and it would seem therefore that they should remain on stage throughout the temptation scene. As this would be theatrically awkward (for they have nothing to say or do for some 350 lines) and as I could remember that they made their exit at this point in the first London production of the play at the Mercury Theatre, I wrote to ask the original producer, Mr. E. Martin Browne, for his views. He replied:

'The play was written for the Chapter House at Canterbury. This was a rectangular room 90 foot long, which at that time had no other door than the one at the back of the auditorium. Thus one could not get actors off in the middle of a scene without stopping the scene for the time it took to get them through 90 feet of close-packed audience. I wrote about this to Eliot when I got Part I, since I realised that the Chorus and Priests would in that hall have to stay on during the Temptations: but he said he had visualised it that way. It does of course correspond (so far as the Chorus is concerned) with the formal Greek pattern in which the play is set; but as you say it involves all these actors in the long misery of having nothing to do (one of the Chorus told us she played the alphabet game with the Tempters' speeches or made up her Christmas-present list—and they did manage to keep alive).

'So, soon after we started at the Mercury, I took the Chorus and Priests off before the First Tempter appeared, bringing them back with "There is no rest in the house"' (line 600).

This all has a bearing on Thomas's line (254)

All things prepare the event. Watch.

Mr. Martin Browne writes:

'I have always read Becket's speech . . . as referring to the temptations to come; not that he expected specifically what comes, but that he is in inner turmoil (the strife with shadows) and feels the struggle becoming more intense at this point. The others sense this, and it makes them afraid of unknown forces, probably of evil, which they feel getting nearer; so they run away in fear, returning when they have failed to find rest elsewhere.'

If we accept this interpretation and the consequent exit of Priests and Chorus (notwithstanding Eliot's original visualisation of the scene), when Thomas says 'Watch', he will not mean 'Watch, here come the Tempters!' but rather 'Watch therefore: for ye know not at what hour your Lord doth come' (Matthew xxiv. 42).

(B) The Tempters would appear from the text to be four aspects of Thomas himself, which, by an effort of will, he discards as untrue to his innermost, real self. One way of bringing this out in production would be to give all four Tempters almost identical masks, modelled to resemble (though with slight ingredients of caricature) the actual face of the actor playing Thomas.

Mr. Martin Browne comments:

'I have tended more and more to interpret the Tempters as exteriorisations of Becket's inner conflicts, present or past ('Voices under sleep, waking a dead world, So that the mind may not be whole in the present'). This follows the line pursued by Eliot in writing the play: he started with the first three as historical figures, then transformed them into the semi-abstract Tempters and added number four.'

The four aspects of Thomas are easily recognised. The first is the natural sensual man who loves pleasure, athletics, music, good company, luxurious fare, gaiety and romance. The second is the man who seeks the exercise of political power and who therefore rebukes Thomas for having resigned the Chancellorship on becoming Archbishop, a great mistake for anyone avid of rule. The third is the man who might have used the power of the Church in secular ways—he is a variation of the second—making cause with the 'people' against the 'throne'. The fourth is the man who seeks the supreme glories of sainthood for the sake of the satisfactions it would bring him, to be able to rule from the tomb and to be 'high in heaven'. This last is the temptation to which we are told Satan succumbed, the temptation to pride. All these four characters are possible Thomases and the fact that they appear to him shows how well he has come to know his own nature and its dangers.

The Fourth Tempter is a surprise not only to Thomas but to the audience, and he offers a temptation they may not have thought of. Thomas says '*I expected three visitors, not four*' (lines 476–7) because Christ was subjected to three, not four, temptations in the wilderness (St. Matthew IV. 1–10) and these three are somewhat parallel to those which Thomas faces, being (1) Temptation to gratify bodily hunger, (2) Temptation to grasp worldly power over 'all the kingdoms of the earth' and (3) Temptation to misuse supernatural power, in Christ's case by performing a showy miracle.

The Fourth Tempter, therefore, comes as a surprise, and it takes longer for Thomas to see through his seductive, but specious, arguments.

(C) It is both convenient and significant to double the parts of the Four Knights with those of the Four Tempters, and this can be suggested (as it was in Mr. Martin Browne's production) by touches of costume. I quote once more from his letter to me:

'Yes, I have always doubled the Tempters and Knights and so far as I can say I should continue to do so if I did the play again. I feel this is an enormous help to the audience in understanding the play. The arguments employed by the three Knights who try to convince the audience have an almost exact correspondence with those of the Tempters 2, 3 and 4 . . . I have for this purpose always wanted the Tempters to show in their costume the characteristics of each . . . the First Knight, who is the only one not to correspond too clearly with his opposite Tempter, acts as Chairman, so does not raise any problem for me.

'. . . I don't see that the mask idea precludes the doubling: indeed I rather think it improves it, for the masks would be paralleled by the nose-pieces of the Knights' helmets. These I didn't have in the original costume but I think they add greatly to the effect of the group. They could be taken off, if desired, for the "Meeting".'

25. (lines 265–71) *Now that you recover favour with the King*. This is the First Tempter's way of referring to the abortive meeting between Thomas and the King, mentioned in Note 11 (to line 97). Henry said that England was not a bush that could hold two such robins (a remark quoted by Dom David Knowles in his masterly essay on Thomas Becket, in his book *The*

Historian and Character (1963)). The Third Tempter is putting a falsely rosy view of the relations between the royal and the archiepiscopal robin. Eliot is careful, it may be noted, to follow history and to insinuate nothing loose about Becket's behaviour in the old days; Becket was famous for his chastity (*Materials*, I, pp. 5–6, and elsewhere) and the cheap suggestions to the contrary in a play about Becket by Monsieur Jean Anouilh are beneath the dignity of the subject, and indeed of M. Anouilh.

26. (line 290) *The wheel on which he turns.* This passage is difficult because Eliot is trying to express metaphysical ideas about the relations between man, Time, Eternity and God, in terms of the image of a wheel. This image dominates the play and constantly recurs to illuminate central meanings. It first appears at line 137, where it implies no more than the turn of temporal events. It reappears more forcefully in lines 216 and 598 (see Introduction, pp. 17–18) and has important bearings on the conclusion of the sermon preached by Thomas (Interlude 61–70). In the present passage Thomas seems to say that all we know of the future in this world is that it will be much like the past: the same seasons will return, year after year, and the same human situations (see Note 3 to line 9). We are caught up in these returning processes and problems inescapably, and to no ultimate purpose, it would seem. Yet if we surrender our wills into harmony with the will of God, cutting ourselves off from 'the love of created beings' (see Introduction, p. 14) and so *sever the cord* (287–8); if we renew our wills, as a snake renews itself by sloughing off its old skin (*shed the scale*), we will evade the meaningless repetitions of the cycles of Time, which only a fool thinks he can himself control (289) and, by uniting our

wills to the will of God at the centre of the wheel,
become a part of that pattern which, since the Incarnation, has given meaning to life.

27. (line 296) *Think of penitence and follow your master.*
Thomas is reminding his visitor (as a priest should) of
penitence and of following the life of Christ, not the life
of pleasure. This is one of the interesting traces of
Eliot's first conception of the Tempters as actual
historical persons visiting him (see Note 24B to line
255): he makes Thomas advise the First Tempter as if he
were an ordinary human being in need of such advice.
A similar trace of Eliot's first conception may be seen
in the lines addressed by Thomas to the Third Tempter:

> For a countryman
> You wrap your meaning in as dark a generality
> As any courtier   (419–21).

28. (line 319) *The impossible is still temptation.* To re-enact
the past is impossible, but one often wishes it were not.
Thomas rejects this way of distracting his attention
from the work before him.

29. (line 324) *We met at Clarendon, at Northampton, and
last at Montmirail.* The Second Tempter tempts
Thomas with the seductions of compromise, of sinking
his differences with the King so as to become, with him,
an all-powerful but benevolent diarchy of King and
Chancellor, dispensing justice and creating a sort of
welfare state by which he would certainly thrive on
earth, and perhaps in heaven as a reward. This
temptation must have been very powerful to Becket,
who loved Henry; some historians think he never loved
anyone else; Fitzstephen (*Materials*, III, p. 25) says
'*Magis unanimes et amici nunquam duo aliqui fuerunt
temporibus Christianis*'. ('No other two in Christian

times were greater friends or more unanimous.') This unanimity and friendship was split by the Constitutions of Clarendon (1164) (where Thomas first met the temptations of compromise in their full strength) and then at Northampton, in the same year, whither the King had summoned him to render account for certain sums of money expended during his Chancellorship; here again he could have done the easier thing and submitted to the King. Lastly in November 1169 at Montmirail (*Materials*, III, p. 446), where another attempt was made to induce Thomas to change his attitude and accept the King's point of view.

30. (line 329) *See how the late ones rise!* Set in a pair of scales against each other, how the memories of these disagreements are weighed down by the weightier and happier memories of Thomas's relations with the King when Chancellor! The Tempter suggests the old amity and power might be regained.

31. (line 341) *With deceitful shadows.* The shadow of pleasure that has just filed past Thomas in the person of the First Tempter and the shadow of allowing himself to be lost in worship, giving love to God alone and so (absorbed by one or other of these shadows) miss the substance of earthly power.

32. (line 345) *A sentence.* The word is used in the mediaeval sense of *sententia*, i.e. an opinion, an aphorism. The *schools* are the schools of disputation in mediaeval universities.

33. (lines 356–9) *Who shall have it?* Compare Sir Arthur Conan Doyle, *The Musgrave Ritual*: '"Whose was it?" "His who is gone." "Who shall have it?" "He who will come." "What was the month?" "The sixth from the first." "Where was the sun?" "Over the oak." "Where was the shadow?" "Under the elm." "How was it

stepped?" "North by ten and ten, east by five and five, south by two and two, west by one and one, and so under." "What shall we give for it?" "All that is ours." "Why should we give it?" "For the sake of the trust."' Eliot's interest in Conan Doyle's work may also be seen in his use of the word *grimpen* in his poem *East Coker*. It is taken from *The Hound of the Baskervilles*.

34. (line 368) *The bishops.* The Archbishop of York, at the King's command, had crowned his son, Henry, in order to secure the succession in advance. The coronation of a King, however, had always been the prerogative of the Archbishop of Canterbury. Becket replied to this infringement of the rights of the See of Canterbury by suspending and excommunicating the Archbishop of York and others, who had assisted him in this (*Materials*, III, pp. 458–9, Herbert of Bosham).

35. (line 378) *Who bind and loose.* This refers to Matthew, xvi, 19, 'And I will give unto thee the keys of the kingdom of heaven: and whatsoever thou shalt bind on earth shall be bound in heaven: and whatsoever thou shalt loose on earth shall be loosed in heaven.' This power was given by Christ to St. Peter (in St. Matthew's words). Later (line 510) the Fourth Tempter tries to encourage Thomas to presume upon it.

36. (line 384) *Covering kings' falcons.* The First and Second Tempters have both appealed to what they believe to be weaknesses in Thomas (love of pleasure, desire to keep friendship with the King and agree on some worldly compromise in power-politics) and these weaknesses, had Thomas yielded to them, would have put him under the King in spiritual matters. But Thomas, in boasting that he keeps the keys of Heaven and Hell (line 376), is guilty of a sin of pride (so the Tempter suggests) that soars up above the lesser sins

Thomas is rejecting, out of the royal sphere of power, into the sphere of God's authority and so he escapes the kinds of temptation offered by the First and Second Tempter: so the Second leaves him to his fate (i.e. the fate of being damned for his 'higher vices', the temptations of which are still to come). The imagery from falconry has an obvious appropriateness to the speaker and his period.

37. (line 389) *But arrest disorder.* i.e. 'only arrest disorder'.

38. (line 390) *Make it fast.* i.e. 'do not allow it food'. The sense of the whole passage is that those who, like King Henry, believe in governing by man-made laws, confident in their ignorance, do not create a true order; they only succeed in putting a brake on disorder and starving it of opportunity; but in doing so they breed a worse disorder unless they are controlled by the order of God, and they degrade justice and righteousness to a merely human conception, a thing for their convenience; to serve the King's law would be a descent from the service of God's law that Becket had undertaken.

39. (line 431) *You and I, my Lord, are Normans.* Thomas's father was a native of Rouen and his mother of Caen. They were both of pure Norman stock. (*Materials*, IV, p. 81.)

40. (line 433) *Let the Angevin.* Henry II was the son of Geoffrey of Anjou (hence Angevin); he had inherited enormous territories in France (Anjou and Maine) and acquired Aquitaine by marrying Eleanor of Aquitaine in 1152. His children were rebellious and he had plenty to occupy him on the continent.

41. (line 447) *Tyrannous jurisdiction.* The Third Tempter's way of describing the attempt of Henry II to establish a single system of law, controlled by the King's Court of Justice, over the whole country, including the Church.

42. (line 462) *In the tilt-yard.* Thomas in his early days was
    a great horseman and skilled in single combat
    (*Materials*, III, p. 35, William Fitzstephen's account).

43. (line 470) *To make, then break, etc.* The Tempter has
    suggested that Thomas has no hope of reconciliation
    with the King (423–4) and that he should ally himself
    with the Barons (445) to break the power of the King,
    whom, in his heart, Thomas still dearly loves (425).
    Thomas rejects this, preferring to trust God only if he
    cannot trust the King any longer (458–9). But to make,
    then break the royal power, though he had thought of
    the possibility before, would in his present circum-
    stances, be the hopeless attempt of a failing man (471)
    and would only achieve what *Samson* achieved *in Gaza*
    (473), when he pulled down the pillars of the house in
    which three thousand of the Philistines had gathered to
    watch him do feats of strength: and so pulled down the
    same destruction on himself (Judges, xvi. 21–30). Yet
    Thomas, were he now to attempt to break the King,
    would fall short of Samson's triumph, and would only
    destroy himself (473).

44. (line 476) *Who are you?* See note to line 255(B), p. 107.

45. (lines 486–501) *Hooks have been baited.* Notice that
    each Tempter in turn annihilates the arguments of the
    Tempter before. Compare lines 338–42 and 422, where
    the Second Tempter derides 'deceitful shadows' (pro-
    posed by the First); and the Third Tempter derides the
    possibility of renewed friendship between Thomas and
    the King (proposed by the Second). The Fourth
    Tempter's speech derides all earlier temptations offered.

46. (line 518) *The Old King.* Henry II was called this after
    his son had been crowned.

47. (line 523 *Supreme, but for one.* The Evil One. Compare
    the last temptation of Christ in the wilderness (Matthew,

iv. 8–9). Thomas does not understand the allusion (though the audience will) and it is not for the Tempter to explain it, since by doing so he would remind Thomas of Christ's example in withstanding the temptation.

48. (line 544) *At the angles of stairs.* A favoured image for indecision in Eliot. Compare *Ash Wednesday*, III.

49. (line 549 and following) *The shrine shall be pillaged.* In this speech Eliot is solving a problem in audience-relationship. A twentieth-century audience, that is, a post-Reformation audience, with a firm belief in progress and a firm rejection of superstition, is likely, even at a Canterbury Festival, to feel quite safe and comfortable, out of the reach of the play's inmost theme of sanctity, and regard the whole performance as a piece of poetical fancy-dress, having, no doubt, some cultural value that may be interesting to discuss later.

> *(In the room the women come and go*
> *Talking of Michelangelo.)*

Eliot, however, wishes the audience to feel the urgency and relevance of sanctity and to undermine their reliance on the superior knowledge they can seem to claim in virtue of the Reformation (when Protestantism put an end to the cult of saints in England) and of their sophisticated interpretations of history. He therefore makes Thomas seem to know (through the mouth of the Fourth Tempter) that a time will come when all the shrines in England will be pillaged (as they were) and St. Thomas will dwindle to a figure about whom a few specialist historians will offer psychological explanations. By thus bringing the play level with the thought of his audience, he diminishes any reliance it may feel in the fact that it all happened hundreds of years ago and that we know better nowadays. They find the Tempter's sneering voice unexpectedly expressing their own thoughts as if they were unanswerable, and yet Thomas finds the answer, and brings it home to them in the speech which ends Part I, especially in its last dozen lines.

It may however seem that the Fourth Tempter, for all his subtlety, is being a little inconsistent. On the one hand he is urging Thomas to snatch at martyrdom for his own personal glory; on the other hand he prophesies a time when there will no longer be any such glory to be snatched. He is really presenting Thomas with two different temptations, both deadly. The first is the blasphemy of using martyrdom and sanctity as a means for his personal glory. The second is to undermine his faith by prophesying a time when all faith will perish. This is a temptation to despair, to what the middle ages called '*wanhope*', a sub-division of the capital sin of sloth or apathy. Thomas feels this in his question 'Is there no enduring crown to be won?' It is not until after long thought that he triumphs over these temptations, and this is dramatically expressed by the long silence into which he falls between lines 600 and 665.

With regard to the prophecy that the time will come when 'men shall declare that there was no mystery' (line 559), no modern historian can accept Eliot's postulate that 'a martyrdom is always the design of God' (Sermon, line 65) because historians wish their art to approximate as nearly as possible to a science, and obey the laws of terrestrial evidence like other scientists. If historians allowed the idea that God from time to time made unaccountable interferences in the course of events, history would cease to be scientific, and so abandon its special discipline, that limits it to the laws of natural evidence. Consequently even those historians who, like Dom David Knowles, are committed by their religious profession to belief in the supernatural and in a divine purpose at work in history manifested at certain moments (supremely at the Incarnation, or in other special cases, as of St. Thomas) must set this kind of belief aside when limiting themselves to the status of historian. So it happens that in his admirable essay, to which I have already referred, Father Knowles plays down the somewhat hagiographical testimony of Becket's friends and contemporaries, remarking that after all they were 'committed to the ultimate sanctity of their subject', whereas he, speaking purely as an historian, is not, whatever he may believe in his larger capacity as a priest.

In the same way a poet is under no obligation to accept the limitations that historians impose on themselves. A poet is concerned to show what can be seen through his eyes, not merely what can be proved in a court of law. Eliot is showing us his vision of the need and nature of sanctity in a politically and materially dominated world, and has found, in the life of Thomas Becket, an example that so exactly embodies his vision that he can declare it without factual misrepresentation of history. All poets tend to be a mixture of *vates* and *artifex*, that is, of prophet and craftsman, man of vision and man of skill. But greatness lies in vision.

50. (line 589) *Can I neither act nor suffer without perdition?* The dilemma in which the Fourth Tempter has placed Thomas is this: if he refuses the temptations to power (pride) offered by the Second and Third Tempters, by choosing martyrdom instead, he is yielding to an even greater sin of pride, the wish to be 'high in heaven'. The

wish to be highest in heaven was the wish of Lucifer which, in Christian thought and imagery, began the perpetual struggle of Good and Evil. Thomas seems to be trapped, and this is emphasised by the ironical repetition of his opening speech: he is faced with having to find a way out of his own paradoxes. While he ponders his difficulty some sixty or seventy lines go by. The stillness of the wheel (line 599) is juxtaposed with the restlessness of the house (line 600). The Four Tempters now unite in a fifth temptation—the temptation to despair, by asserting that everything is vanity and illusion anyhow; the Priests add their cowardly entreaties, and there is a litany of apprehension and nameless terror from the Chorus. Tempters, Priests and Chorus unite in pressing a craven decision on Thomas. But he suddenly sees the way out of the trap. If he can neither act nor suffer by willing to do so on the human plane (i.e. by a self-regarding action or suffering) without being damned for the sin of pride, he can give his will into the will of God, for 'in His will lies our peace', as Dante says (*Paradiso*, Canto III, line 85). In much the same way Everyman, at the hour of his death, commends his soul into the hands of God, using the words of Christ on the cross: *In manus tuas commendo spiritum meum* (Luke, XXIII. 46).

51. (line 607 onwards) *The Catherine wheel, the pantomime cat, etc.* Here the Four Tempters step out of the twelfth century into the twentieth, for the benefit of the audience, as they do again later when they take the forms of the Four Knights and address their sardonic political apology to their spectators. In the present passage they talk in terms of our own times, using homely images of things which turn out to be less glorious than they seem, so as to shock the audience

into a sharper sense of awareness of and familiarity with the situation before them. They are putting forward the dejecting view that prizes are not worth winning anyhow and that the hope of martyrdom is no better than a hankering for the cat in the pantomime, which isn't a cat at all, but just another cheat. This is the temptation to *wanhope*, mentioned in the note to line 549. It is now being offered, not only to Thomas, but also to the audience, so that they, by adopting the Tempters' point of view, may despise Thomas as someone who is still the victim of childish illusions and 'out of touch with reality'. So once again the audience is brought back with a jolt to ask itself what 'reality' really is? It is brought back to Prufrock's 'overwhelming question', which worries Sweeney too. Which are more *real*, material things like the pride of power (motor-cars, etc., etc.) or spiritual things like self-sacrificing love and a purified will?

52. (line 624 *et seq.*) *Is it the owl that calls.* In this passage the technique of an alternation of speakers, each capping the other line by line, is imitated from Greek tragedy, and is known as stichomythia. The imagery of prowling presences and of our nearness to death increases the atmosphere of anxiety with nightmare terrors. Death is the Stranger that everyone has to face, and before whom all things crumble except a will made perfect, as *The Rock* suggests.

53. (line 638) *We know of oppression and torture.* The *Peterborough Chronicle*, a contemporary record of the days of King Stephen, to whom Henry II succeeded, tells of the 'untellendliche pynes' or unspeakable tortures to which many were put by lawless brigand-barons in the dungeons of their castles, to extort the secret of where they had hidden their money.

54. (line 659 onwards) *Puss-purr of leopard, etc.* More
    images to produce a general terror, that use nature to
    give a sense of the unnatural. It is the moment of crisis.
55. (line 669) *Venial sin.* Sin that is pardonable, not mortal
    or deadly. A man who died in deadly sin, unrepented
    and unconfessed, was held to have incurred damnation.
    The deadly or 'Head-Sins' are Pride, Envy, Anger,
    Lust, Gluttony, Avarice and Sloth. Chaucer, in his
    Parson's Tale, tells us 'soothly whan man loveth any
    creature moore than Jhesu Crist oure Creatour, thanne
    is it deadly synne. And venial synne is it, if man love
    Jhesu Crist lasse than hym oghte. For sooth is that if a
    man yeve his love, the which he oweth al to God with al
    his herte, unto a creature, certes as much of his love as
    he yeveth to thilke creature, so much he bireaveth fro
    God'. This may be compared with the epigraph on the
    title-page of *Sweeney Agonistes*, already quoted (see
    Introduction, p. 14). Thomas is recalling the 'natural
    vigour' of our self-interest in the pursuit of pleasure
    and self-advancement that is with us from birth, and
    often leads a man into loving Christ 'lasse than hym
    oghte'; a venial sin pursued may easily lead to the
    deadly one of rejecting the love of Christ for 'the love
    of created beings'.
56. (line 671 and onwards) *Thirty years ago, etc.* Thomas
    recapitulates the work of the Four Tempters as he sees
    it, looking back into his former life: he perceives the
    deep truth that *sin grows with doing good* (682) because
    in resisting sin you may open your heart to the pride of
    having resisted it and to the contempt of those who
    have not (685), forgetting God (688), though still useful
    to society (692), and so making the purpose of life a
    merely political thing, not something sanctified and
    holy in its dedication, a limited, natural objective

instead of an infinite supernatural one: to do this is no doubt well enough, but it means ignoring 'the overwhelming question' that Prufrock wanted to ask. Thomas sees that martyrdom lies before him and that by patiently accepting it (as he must and will) he will seem, in the eyes of those who cannot understand a saint's surrender to God, to be performing an act of futile and *senseless self-slaughter*, the action of a *lunatic* (697). And indeed this is precisely the interpretation put upon it by the Fourth Knight (who is also the Fourth Tempter) when he suggests that Thomas committed *Suicide while of Unsound Mind* (Part II, 574).

The conclusion reached by Thomas is that

> *history at all times draws*
> *The strangest consequence from remotest cause* (700).

He means that God can draw good out of evil; the murder of Thomas is evil, yet its consequences (in renewing the worship of God in the hearts of men) will be good. Yet this does not mean that the sin of the Four Knights, their *sacrilege* (701), will go unpunished. All four of them

> *You, and you*
> *And you, must all be punished. So must you.*

By resisting the Tempters, Thomas has made perfect his will, *to the sword's end* (705) and he is therefore at peace within himself, so action and suffering are over for him: as he says later (Part II, 260–62)

> *Death will only come when I am worthy,*
> *And if I am worthy, there is no danger.*
> *I have therefore only to make perfect my will.*

This peace of mind he has achieved is reflected in his

sermon which immediately follows. It is peace indeed, but '*not peace as the world gives*' (Sermon, line 40).

INTERLUDE

1. *Glory to God in the highest. Materials*, III, p. 130. In the account given by William Fitzstephen, this text (Luke, II. 14) was that on which Becket preached his last sermon, on Christmas night, 1170. It need hardly be said that this sermon, as Eliot has imagined it, is the core of his vision of sanctity. To understand this sermon, in its application to the action and discourse as a whole, is to understand the play.

2. (lines 29–30) *My peace I give unto you* . . . (line 39) *Not as the world gives*. . . . See John, XIV. 27.

3. (line 68) *Who has lost his will in the will of God*. Cf. Dante, *Paradiso*, Canto III, line 85:

   E'n la sua voluntate è nostra pace
   (And in his will is our peace).

4. (line 78) *Archbishop Elphege* . . . . *in a short time you may have yet another martyr. Materials*, III, p. 130: William Fitzstephen: 'he said that they had one martyr-Archbishop, St. Elphege; it was possible they would have another in a short time.' St. Elphege (or Alphege) properly called Aelfeah, lived between A.D. 954 and 1012, and became Archbishop of Canterbury in 1006. The Danes sacked Canterbury in 1011, and barbarously murdered him on 19th April, 1012, at Greenwich, for refusing to pay them a ransom.

PART II

Part II originally opened with lines 28–63: in the second edition (1936) the chorus which now opens Part II was substituted. In the third edition the lines were included in an Appendix (1937) and in the present edition, in which the text of the Fourth edition is followed, they come after the chorus, as a permanent part of the text.

The three Priests mark the passage of the three days after Christmas that were also the three days before the murder of Thomas: they were the feasts of St. Stephen, of St. John and of the Holy Innocents. Their entry, one after the other, each using the same formula of speech, gives that sense of ritual which Eliot accepted as one of the tap-roots of drama, an idea largely derived from his study of F. M. Cornford and the great Greek dramatists.

An *Introit* is a variable part of the Mass, composed of a versicle or sentence with phrases taken from the psalms, or elsewhere in the Bible, said or sung, as the priest approaches the altar to celebrate the Eucharist.

1. (line 29) *Princes moreover did sit, and did witness falsely against me.* Psalm 119, v. 23: Princes also did sit and speak against me. Mark, XIV, 56: For many bore false witness against him.

2. (line 35) *In the midst of the congregation he opened his mouth.* Psalm 22, v. 22: In the midst of the congregation will I praise thee.

3. (line 36) *That which was from the beginning . . . declare we unto you.* 1 John, I. 1: That which was from the beginning, which we have heard, which we have seen with our eyes, which we have looked upon, and our hands have handled, of the Word of life . . . that which we have seen and heard declare we unto you.

4. (line 42) *Out of the mouth of very babes.* Psalm 8. 2: Out of the mouth of babes and sucklings hast thou ordained strength because of thine enemies. . . .

5. (line 44) *They sung as it were a new song.* Psalm 96. 1: O sing unto the Lord a new song.

6. (line 45) *The blood of thy saints.* Psalm 79. 2–3: They have given . . . the flesh of thy saints unto the beasts of the earth. Their blood have they shed like water round about Jerusalem.

7. (line 46) *No man to bury them.* Psalm 79. 3: Their blood have they shed like water round about Jerusalem; and there was none to bury them.

8. (lines 46–7) *Avenge, O Lord, the blood of they saints.* Deuteronomy, XXXII, 43: Rejoice, o ye nations, with his people: for he will avenge the blood of his servants. Compare Milton, Sonnet *On the late Massacre in Piedmont,* 'Avenge, O Lord, thy slaughtered Saints.'

9. (line 47) *In Rama, a voice heard, weeping.* Matthew, II. 18. In Rama was there a voice heard, lamentation and weeping, and great mourning, Rachel weeping for her children and would not be comforted, because they are not.

10. (line 50) *Rejoice we all, keeping holy day.* Psalm 42, v. 4: In the voice of praise and thanksgiving: among such as keep holy-day.

11. (line 52) *He lays down his life for the sheep.* John, X. 14–15: I am the good shepherd and know my sheep, and am known of mine. As the Father knoweth me, even so know I the Father: and I lay down my life for the sheep.

12. (line 54) *To-day, what is to-day?* This passage plunges us back into the seemingly inescapable cycle of Time, in which 'one moment weighs like another' (58–9); but when we look back on the past we are able to pick out our great moments, and are able to say '*that was the day*' (60). But in fact any moment may be such a moment of miracle, here and now, because *now* is the ever-present moment in which the decisive thing may happen, and reveal the 'pattern' (see Part I, line 215). The present is

that moment in Time in which timeless Eternity can present itself to our awareness.

13. (line 63) *Servants of the King. Materials*, III, p. 132 (William Fitzstephen) 'Our Lord the King has sent us.'

14. (line 75) *Please dine with us. Materials*, II, p. 430 (Edward Grim) 'They (the Knights) were met with honour, as servants of the king, and well known. They are invited to table. . . .' The First Knight's un-mannerly reply about pork (78–9) is obviously a crude joke about the intended murder of Thomas. They will first kill him and then dine out upon the story afterwards.

15. (line 87) *Matters of other urgency*. See *Materials*, I, pp. 115–20, where a number of matters connected with the See of Canterbury and what had happened to it during Thomas's exile, are listed as occupying his attention. He has put *the papers in order* (89) so that all shall have been seen to and completed before his death.

16. (line 107) *Saving my order*. The phrase that Becket, from the beginning of the quarrel, had used to imply that his first duty, as Archbishop, was to God, and only after that had he a duty to the King. Nothing that conflicted with the first loyalty could be due to the second. This his enemies considered a quibble. The 'order' referred to is, of course, Holy Orders, which will not save him from assassination. *Materials*, III, p. 273.

17. (line 115) *Yes, we'll pray for you!* The repetition of this half-line is a trick of satirical versification that first appears in Eliot's *Sweeney Agonistes*.

> *Doris*. I'll convert you! *Sweeney*. I'll convert *you* into a stew!

It is also used in *The Cocktail Party*.

> *Alex*. He was feeble-minded.
> *Julia*.   Oh, not feeble-minded,
> He was only harmless.

18. (line 129) *If you make charges*. According to William of Canterbury (*Materials*, I, p. 129) and to the Anonymous Author I (*Materials*, IV, p. 71), what actually happened was that the Knights asked if he would wish their interview with him to be held in public or in private, and he replied 'As you wish'. Thomas's attendants, all but the door-keeper, then left and Fitz Urse began to put forward certain of the King's commands. Thomas said 'These words should not be kept secret' and sent the door-keeper to fetch the monks back. Eliot has condensed the incident.

19. (line 153) *Evince*. Overcome.

20. (line 165) *As for the bishops*. '"In any case," said Reginald, "it was thanks to you that the Bishops were excommunicated: and therefore it is our Lord the King's wish that you should absolve them speedily." "I don't deny," said the holy man, "that it was thanks to me, but it was not *by* me, and so unless they first present themselves to the Pope, who passed the sentence on them, with due humility and satisfaction rendered, they haven't the least chance of being absolved by me"' (*Materials*, IV, p. 72, Anonymous Author I). The same authority is cited in line 175, *That you and your servants depart from this land*. 'Then Reginald with fury said, "The King therefore commands you to leave his lands quickly and without delay, with all your foreign clerics and all those who belong to you."'

21. (line 197) *Malfeasance*. A word meaning *evil-doing* (from the French *malfaisant*) mainly used in law, to apply to 'official misconduct on the part of one in public employment' (*Oxford English Dictionary*).

22. (line 199) *But if you kill me*. '"I know that you have come to kill me, but I make God my shield", rapidly

tapping his forehead with his hand. "Here," he said, "Here you will find me!"' (*Materials*, IV, p. 73).

23. (line 202) *Restrain this man.* 'Then the Knights left, vehemently threatening the archbishop and uttering warnings on behalf of the king that he was to be carefully guarded, lest he escape' (*Ibid.*, p. 73).

24. (line 205) *I have smelt them, et seq.* In this Chorus, as in that from Part I, lines 656–62, the images are chosen to suggest horror, nausea, hysteria, monstrousness, brute-beastliness; then death in things beautiful, corruption in food, the jungle and the sea-bottom. The effect is to extend the power of evil to universal dimensions, and not simply to limit it to a handful of rude and brawling knights with some shadowy king behind them. If the making of a martyr is a thing in which God directly acts, then the hosts of Hell may be imagined as rising up against it; we are witnessing something more cosmic than a church-and-state squabble. It is a poetry of terror and disgust, intended to turn your stomach over. Images of this kind depend for their effectiveness on non-rational, private associations of idea. Many, for instance, eat oysters ('smooth creatures still living, with the strong taste of salt') without disgust, and few will be able to imagine the smell of death in a holly-hock. But in this tremendous aggregate of things intended to convey an imminence of evil, there is hope that *every* image will strike *some* members of every audience, with a sick anticipation of the abomination about to take place. It is difficult to create an imagery of evil out of the innocent works of Nature. What is wrong, or stomach-turning, in a sea-anemone? Some may feel a sub-conscious repugnance, others not. There is a painting by Breughel of the Fall of the Angels, in which the angels, as they fall, turn into insects: but

these include many gorgeous butterflies, and those of us who feel no horror on seeing a butterfly (a majority, I suppose) may even think these fallen angels more beautiful than before, and certainly as harmless. To find the irresistible image is the perpetual quest of poetry, and in describing the supernatural, we only have the natural to draw on, the seen for the unseen.

25. (line 237) *I have consented.* The acknowledgment of guilt, of having partaken in guilt in cruelty by 'flirting with the passage of the kite' in cowardice by having 'cowered with the wren' and by self-identification with the horror in these images of horror, is made by the Chorus to incite the self-identification of the audience with it. That ritual purgation is at the root of drama, as re-conceived by Eliot from Greek patterns, is evident from this chorus as it is from the last chorus of *The Rock*.

26. (line 238) *Torn away.* Perhaps torn away from Thomas and from the faith that supports him so strongly. The difficult phrases in the following lines '*United to the spiritual flesh of nature, mastered by the animal powers of spirit*' seem once again to point to a cosmic overturning, and some critics, particularly David E. Jones, see the situation as one of 'pervasive disorder in the natural world'. It is a disorder which, he suggests, persists in man 'as Original Sin'.

'Man turns his back on God and becomes mere animal, for when he forgets the fatherhood of God, he has nothing left but his brotherhood with the beast. . . . The link between the animal creation (man is both intellect as angels are, and sense as animals are) is broken and disorder rules in the natural world' (*The Plays of T. S. Eliot*, pp. 75–6, by D. E. Jones, 1960). Eliot begins the chorus under discussion with the sentence

128

> I have smelt them, the death-bringers, senses are
> quickened
> By *subtile* forebodings. (my italics)

This spelling *subtile* for *subtle* is taken from John Donne's poem *The Ecstasie,* where it occurs thus:

> As our blood labours to beget
> Spirits as like souls as it can,
> Because such fingers need to knit
> The subtile knot which makes us man.

and the allusion to 'the spiritual flesh of nature, mastered by the animal powers of the spirit' refer to the 'spirits' here mentioned in Donne's poem. The nature of *spirit*, as understood by Donne and the middle ages, is a kind of emanation within us from our animal bodies and bloods; they are 'just sufficiently material for them to act upon the body, but so very fine and attenuated that they could be acted upon by the wholly immaterial soul' (C. S. Lewis, *The Discarded Image*, 1964, p. 167). The lines under discussion in *Murder in the Cathedral* mean that a reversal of the natural order is taking place, and the *spirit* that should be acted on by the soul, and so act upon the body, is in fact being acted on by bodily lust and so the soul is unable to act upon it. The hierarchy of things is going into reverse.

27. (line 243) *By the final ecstasy of waste and shame.* An allusion to and echo of Shakespeare's 129th sonnet, that begins

> The expense of spirit in a waste of shame
> Is lust in action. . . .

28. (line 247) *The eternal burden, the perpetual glory.* Compare Thomas's Sermon, lines 55–60. Some truths can only be expressed and apprehended in paradox.

Paradox is a way of thinking much used by Christ and by St. Paul. Truth is revealed in the flash of contraries.

29. (line 258) *My Lord, you must not stop here.* 'Then the monks, many of whom were present, said to him "My Lord, go into the church"' (*Materials*, III, p. 138, William Fitzstephen). They hurried him off by force.

30. (line 262) *I have therefore only to make perfect my will.* Cf. *The Rock*, quoted in the Introduction, p. 16.

31. (line 278 *et seq.*) *The Dies Irae*, which means the Day of Wrath, is the name of a hymn attributed to Thomas of Celano (*c.* 1200–1255). It is one of the great master-pieces of mediaeval lyric poetry. The rhythmic form of the three verses (lines 279–87) that start the chorus and of the two (lines 304–9) that end it, is imitated from it. These last two verses are rough translations from the *Dies Irae*, and appear thus in the original:

> Quaerens me, sedisti lassus,
> Redemisti crucem passus;
> Tantus labor non sit cassus.
>
> Oro supplex et acclinis,
> Cor contritum quasi cinis.
> Gere curam mei finis.

(Seeking me, thou didst sink exhausted, thou didst redeem me, having suffered the cross: let not so great a labour be in vain.

I pray, a suppliant, leaning on thee, my heart consumed as it were a cinder. Do thou have care over my ending.)

32. (line 292) *And behind the Judgement the Void.* These are the fears, not of Thomas, but of the Chorus, leaderless without him and shaken by the imminence of death. They are thinking of the Last Four Things, Death,

Judgment, Hell and Heaven, but especially, in their terror, of the first three of these. *The Void* is Hell itself, here conceived as *emptiness, absence, separation from God* (293) which is more terrible even than the *active shapes of Hell* (292), such as artists and poets have pictured, for instance in the many mediaeval paintings of the Day of Judgment that adorned the walls of churches (as in the church of South Leigh, Oxfordshire) or in the *Inferno* of Dante. Eliot's *void* is imagined as a state of being in which the soul can take no comfort of any kind, being perpetually confronted by the knowledge of its own nothingness, and its solitude in nothingness. Compare the close of *Ash Wednesday* (p. 13).

33. (line 303) *Who intercede for me, in my most need?* The first half of this line is from the *Dies Irae* ('*Quem patronum rogaturus?*' On what patron shall I call?) and the second half is from *Everyman*, 'Have mercy on me in this most need.'

34. (line 310) *Bar the door.* The monks locked the cathedral doors but Becket commanded them to open them again. This is vouched for by several eye-witness authorities, e.g. The Anonymous Authors I and II (*Materials*, IV, pp. 75 and 129) and William Fitzstephen (*Materials*, III, p. 139).

35. (line 318) *Turned into a fortress.* 'Far be it from me to make a castle of the Church of God: let all come in that wish to, and God's will be done!' (*Materials*, III, p. 139. William Fitzstephen.)

36. (line 339) *It is not in time that my death shall be known.* Thomas's argument is that when an act is looked at in Time, it can be assessed relatively to its motives and consequences, that is, it is a human action that partakes of both good and evil, as the world judges. To murder a man, not to say an Archbishop, is judged evil by the

world, and therefore it would seem wrong for Becket to make such a murder possible by opening the doors. But if a martyrdom is 'made by the design of God', it is an act made beyond Time, and bears an eternal witness. It is absolute and cannot be judged relatively. Becket's will is only involved in that he has identified it with, or surrendered it to, the will of God.

37. (line 355) *Come down Daniel to the lions' den.* This and the following lines are written in allusion to a jazz-rhythm revivalistic poem by the American poet Vachel Lindsay, called *Daniel Jazz*, published in 1920.

38. (lines 356–7) *The mark of the beast . . . the blood of the Lamb.* A mocking allusion to Revelations, XIX. 20 and VII. 14. Thomas has already alluded to the former in saying

> *We have fought the beast and conquered* (347–8).

He means that he has fought the evil of the Tempters and has overcome it. Compared with the anguish of his effort against temptation, the anguish of martyrdom is easier to endure.

39. (line 382) *Do with me as you will, etc.* Compare *Materials*, IV, page 131, Anonymous Author II:

> 'Si caput', inquit, 'meum vultis, ex parte Dei per anathema prohibeo ne quemquam meorum tangatis.'
> ('If it is my head', he said, 'that you want, on God's behalf, I forbid you by anathema to touch any of my people.')

40. (line 388) *As my temporal vassal.* Fitz Urse was, feudally speaking, a man of Becket's, having received benefits from him in earlier days, so he hated him the more: 'When Reginald son of Urse, who first laid hands on him, pressed more vehemently upon him, the

man of God, shaking himself free, flung him from him, so that he almost fell on the pavement, and said to him "Get out of here: you are my man, and ought not to touch me"'(*Materials*, IV, p. 76, Anonymous Author I).

41. (line 393) *Now to Almighty God....* Becket's last words almost exactly as given by William Fitzstephen, *Materials*, III, p. 141, and Anonymous Authors I and II, Vol. IV, pp. 77 and 131.

42. (line 396) *While the Knights kill him.* This must not be done naturalistically, but as part of a deliberate ritual, like a slow and symbolic ballet-movement. Thomas should be at the centre of a wheel the spokes of which are the swords of the Knights.

43. (line 397) *Clear the air!* In this Chorus of wild protest and amazement at the pollution of the natural order, all sense of Time and Place is lost and the immensity of cosmic evil overwhelms these poor women of Canterbury, who are accustomed only to coping with their daily and parochial troubles, of which they can thankfully say 'Sufficient to the day is the evil thereof'. But what they now suffer is universal, an abomination beyond imagination, endurance and redress: the world itself is wholly fouled, beyond anything that is possible for them to do to cleanse it; so they call for impossibilities, such as cleaning the sky or washing the wind or the brain. (The idea of 'washing the brain' must of course not be confused with 'brain-washing', the name now given to a process of political indoctrination. *Murder in the Cathedral* was written many years before this horrible thing was thought of.)

The *barren boughs* that bleed when broken (line 400) recall the suicides that appeared to Dante in Hell as trees, that bled if you broke their branches (*Inferno*, Canto XIII).

The soft quiet seasons (401); Compare Part I, 9–47.

An instant eternity (418). The idea of a perpetual instant is another paradox to express a thought we cannot think directly. Our language is constructed to cope with our normal existence, as we apprehend it through our physical senses, in Time and Space. We use prepositions like through, in, under, before, after, above, that relate to three-dimensional things, and to the past, present and future of Time, in which we seem to live. But we have intuitions of modes of being that cannot be expressed in these simple terms: we live in Space but we have intuitions of Infinity: we live in Time, but have intuitions of Eternity. Infinity does not simply mean more and more and more Space, any more than Eternity just means more and more and more Time. The phrase *instant eternity* is meant to convey what an ephemeral Time-conditioned creature can, for a split second, apprehend and endure of absolute reality, of 'the perpetual struggle of Good and Evil'. But, as Thomas says (Part II, line 257), 'Human kind cannot bear very much reality.'

44. (line 422 onwards) *The Knights . . . address the audience.* Something has already been said in the Introduction of this unusual feature (p. 19). Soliloquy, in which the speaker directly addresses his audience, is the most powerful instrument of discourse in the playwright's hand: if Hamlet is the most famous figure in world theatre, it is largely because of his soliloquies. During the nineteenth century, the invention of the picture-frame stage and of the master-switch (by which the stage could be isolated from the audience by lighting) favoured the rather childish stage-effects of 'naturalism' so it not only became fashionable to write plays limited to what could 'actually happen' in 'real life',

but also to decry soliloquy and direct address, because in 'real life' we do not talk to ourselves, and have no audience to address. The imbecilities of 'naturalism' are however based in a confusion between what is art and what is nature; a work of art makes its appeal not to what is possible or to be met with in every-day experience, but to what is *imaginable*; it transcends the limits of every-day experience; just as the medium of painting can present the imagination with impressions and abstractions, so that of theatre can present it with discourse other than that taken from normal conversation. Eliot's use of direct address in these speeches is a striking innovation in the theatrical technique of its time.

Nevertheless the Knights speak in a highly natural-istic and coloquial twentieth-century style, even if they suddenly turn a theatre into a political meeting. They have a highly skilled mastery of *cliché*—they tell us we are Englishmen and believe in fair play, that our sympathies are with the under-dog, that we insist on hearing both sides of the case, that they are inexperienced in public speaking, that they are getting nothing out of what they have done, that the arch-bishop put up a jolly good show, that we won't be taken in by emotional clap-trap, that he was, after all, a very great man, and so on.

The tag about our long-established principle of Trial by Jury (431–2) is another of these *clichés*. Trial by Jury was introduced by Henry II himself, with other legal reforms, and was quite recent.

The two best speeches are those of the Second and Fourth Knight, for although the others make their points and are diverting enough, these two put the historical situation with so great a show of fairness that many modern historians would agree with them. The passages beginning at lines 494 and 553 offer a tenable view that sounds quite reasonable; but the brute fact is that such views led to murder and sacrilege. The idea that the Archbishop committed suicide would be more plausible if the audience had not heard Becket's Sermon.

45. (line 589) *Their world without God.* Compare *The Rock*, opening chorus.

46. (lines 602–3) *To share his filthy rites.* The Third Priest may be excused for not knowing very much about the religion of Islam, which has no filthy rites, and is indeed an ascetic, warrior religion, and shares the Old Testament scriptures with Christianity. Saracens were followers of the Prophet, and were forbidden wine. *Libidinous courts* is therefore another slander on them.

47. (line 610) *Pacing forever in the hell of make-believe.* The Third Priest seems to take pleasure in the fate of the murderers. It is hard for those who are not saints to forgive their enemies.

48. (line 640) *The loneliness of the night of God.* An idea recalling *The Ascent of Mt. Carmel* by St. John of the Cross:

'We may say that there are three reasons for which this journey made by the soul to union with God is called night. The first has to do with the point from which the soul goes forth, for it has gradually to deprive itself of desire for all the worldly things which it possessed, by denying them to itself; the which denial and deprivation are, as it were, night to all the senses of man. The second reason has to do with the mean, or the road along which the soul must travel to this union—that is, faith, which is likewise as dark as night to the understanding. The third has to do with the point to which it travels—namely God, Who, equally, is dark night to the soul in this life . . .' (*The Complete Works of St. John of the Cross*, translated and edited by E. Allison Peers, in 3 volumes, 1947, Vol. I, pp. 19–20).

Appendices

I

BRIEF SYNOPSIS OF THE
HISTORICAL SITUATION

Thomas Becket was born in London, of Norman parents, towards the year 1118. He was educated at Merton Priory and later in London and Paris. At the age of 22 he returned to England and became a notary to a rich relation, Osbert Deniers. In about 1142 he attracted the notice of Theobald, Archbishop of Canterbury, whose clerk he then became, rising to the position of Archdeacon of Canterbury in 1154, when he was about 36 years old. So able did he seem that in the following year King Henry appointed him Chancellor of the realm. This was a post of highest importance, and carried a power second only to that of the King. Becket and the King seemed fast friends; it is said that Henry was the only person Becket is known to have loved. Henry was twenty-two when he created Becket Chancellor; Becket threw himself into his work with excitement and efficiency, and lived with lavish splendour and enjoyment, hunting, hawking, tilting and entertaining: all the authorities report him to have been indefatigable and incorruptible in his office and equable and friendly in manner to all; he was noted also for his strict chastity in the easy-going environment of the Court.

In view of all these qualities and the co-operative service he had given him, Henry advanced him in 1162 to the Archbishopric of Canterbury; Becket reluctantly accepted the post, while insisting upon relinquishing his Chancellorship; he warned Henry that as Archbishop he would have other loyalties that might bring him into opposition to the King. Henry disregarded this objection, thinking it a formality.

During the anarchy of the previous reign of King Stephen, when all law was, if not in abeyance, highly unreliable, the Church had taken into its own care the trial of criminal clergy: the worst penalty the Church could inflict was to unfrock the criminal: consequently a cleric who committed a murder and was convicted in a Church Court, was virtually left unpunished for it, compared, at least, to what a layman would have suffered for such a crime. King Henry was anxious to have a uniform, secular authority in matters of justice established over the whole country, clerics included: and he claimed that such a system had in fact existed until the anarchy of Stephen had destroyed it. He was determined to restore the 'ancient customs' of the kingdom in this respect, and to exert more control over clerics, especially in this matter, and in the matter of appeals and visits to Rome in search of papal backing in Church affairs. He wanted no interference in his system of government.

He therefore drew up a statement of some sixteen points to define exactly the relations between Church and State; these were the famous 'Constitutions' which he presented for acceptance at Clarendon in 1164. The Bishops demurred; Becket opposed. No one, he said, should be punished twice for the same offence; to unfrock a priest and then to hang him was to punish him twice. After much pressure, he was persuaded to sign his consent. But he declined to seal it, and did penance for his signature by fasting and abstaining from serving at the Altar. We may imagine the effect of Becket's opposition backed by these ascetic rigours in terms of Gandhi's in more recent times; these two great men had much in common, particularly in their power to combine saintly self-denial with legal acuity.

The King, for all his anger, went about his counter-attack with caution. He resolved to indict him for secular offences and accused him of having denied justice, and of having failed to produce certain accounts, alleged to have been due from him as Chancellor. Becket was summoned to meet these charges at Northampton towards the end of that year (1164). Becket fell sick. The King accused him of shamming. In the end Becket appeared, bearing his cross before him as a protection. The King demanded his assent to the Constitutions. Becket appealed to the Pope. The King claimed £30,000 from him in respect of moneys which he said were due from the time of Becket's Chancellorship. The Archbishop's imprisonment was resolved upon; but Becket was too quick for his sometime friend. He fled by night from a friendly abbey and escaped to Flanders; it was in November 1164. Henry pressed the King of France for his extradition; King Louis declined it on the ground that 'he had not fled because of having committed a crime, but because he feared violence'. The Pope, at Becket's entreaty, condemned the Constitutions. A sort of stalemate ensued; Becket took up residence in the Burgundian monastery of Pontigny, and for some years Henry and he remained in feud, each manoeuvring for whatever continental support he was able to command, or inveigle. The years and the negotiations dragged on inconclusively.

In time Henry's thoughts turned to other problems; he had become anxious about the succession to his throne, and felt it might help to secure it to his eldest son, Prince Henry, if he could arrange for him to be crowned while he himself was still alive and King. In 1170 he persuaded the Archbishop of York, together with the Bishops of London and Salisbury, to officiate at this advance-coronation. It had, however, from time immemorial, been claimed as the right of the See of Canterbury to crown the Kings of

England; Becket, seeing his rights infringed, instantly suspended the Archbishop of York and his co-adjutors, and persuaded the Pope to confirm their suspension. After further negotiation, the Pope brought pressure to bear on Henry to effect a reconcilement, and the King met Becket at Fréteval on 22 July, 1170. A sort of truce was achieved, but as no mention was made between them of the Constitutions of Clarendon, and as King Henry refused his friend the formal kiss of peace, it meant no more than a lull between eruptions.

Becket (it is reported by William of Canterbury) had earlier had a vision of his martyrdom—'Lo! Four of the King's satellites rushing in upon me, broke the crown of my head with swords. What does this vision portend if not the end of my labours?' He determined to return to England and to Canterbury. The Dean of Boulogne warned him not to: 'There are those ready who are after your life,' he said. 'Believe me,' answered Becket, 'not if I were to be torn asunder, limb by limb, would I relinquish this journey. Let it suffice that the Lord's flock has mourned the absence of their shepherd seven years.' He reached Canterbury in time to preach his Christmas sermon, for the year 1170. He was murdered on the twenty-ninth of December, on the steps going down towards the transept, on the north side of his cathedral, by Fitz Urse, de Traci, de Morville and Brito.

II

THE METRE OF *EVERYMAN*

Eliot has told us that in fashioning the verse of *Murder in the Cathedral* he kept in mind the versification of *Everyman*, hoping that anything unusual in the sound of it would be, on the whole, advantageous. An avoidance of too much iambic, some use of alliteration, and occasional unexpected rhyme, 'helped to distinguish the versification' (of his own play) 'from that of the nineteenth century' (*Poetry and Drama*, 1951, p. 24).

Everyman is a version, from the late fifteenth century, of a Dutch original called *Elckerlijc*. It tells of how God, perceiving that 'all people be to me unkind', sends Death to summon Everyman before him: he is to bring his Book of Accounts with him. Everyman begs for a respite and tries to persuade his Friends, his Kinsmen and his Goods to go with him, but they all refuse. His Good-Deeds, however, is willing to stand by him, through death and after. Everyman confesses his sins, takes the last Sacrament, and creeps into the grave to die. Thereupon an Angel announces 'great joy and melody' above in Heaven, 'where Everyman's soul received shall be'.

Its versification is extremely irregular, at least in comparison with that of the earlier Miracle and Morality plays, which, nevertheless, it partly imitates.

The lines are of varying length and have a varying number of stresses: there is a good deal of rhyme and there are touches of alliteration. The way to feel for its rhythms is to stress the most important syllables of the most important words, and let the rest trip along on the tongue, with a slight breath-pause at the ends of lines, where it may seem necessary, and a slight marking of the rhymes, where they occur. Now and then there are words which have dropped out of the language since the fifteenth century, but the best way with them is to pronounce them boldly and hope that the audience (which usually listens to gists rather than to words) will have no trouble in guessing their meaning. The changes in the language have also affected some of the rhymes; for instance in the following passage:

> What and I to Fellowship thereof spake
> And showed him of this sudden chance?
> For in him is all my affiance.

In the fifteenth century they stressed the last syllable of affiance thus: affi*ance*. And so it made a perfect rhyme with *chance*. But now we say af*fi*ance and the rhyme is lost.

But whether we read *Everyman* in the fifteenth- or in the twentieth-century manner, it yields a kind of verse-movement quite different in its effect from that of iambic blank verse; it is specially different in having the pleasing, natural jerkiness of conversation with its sudden surprises, while retaining a certain arbitrary rhythm or balance, helped by the emphases of rhyme. Because everything depends on the variable stresses we naturally put on words and their meaning, there may be many secondary stresses, and the precise weight and balance given to a line will vary with the speaker. It is impossible to represent more than crudely the flow of the rhythms in *Everyman*, but I offer a passage as a sample, showing by italics roughly how I think it should be spoken; main stresses are indicated by acute accents and secondary stresses by grave accents. The passage is taken from the dialogue between *Everyman* and *Death* towards the beginning of the play, when *Death* summons *Everyman* to prepare himself to appear before God for judgment:

The Metre of 'Everyman'

Death :   *Sée* thou make thee *reády* | *shór*tly,

For thou *máy*est | *sáy* || *thís* is the *dáy*

When *nó* | *mán* | *lív*ing | shall *scápe* awáy.

Everyman :   Alás! I may *wéll* | *wéep* || with *síghs* | *déep*

Nów have I *nó mán*ner of *cóm*pany

To *hélp* me in my *jóur*ney | and *mé* to *kéep*;

*Á*lso my *wrít*ing is *fúll* unreády.

Hów shall I do *now* | for to ex*cúse* me?

I would to *Gód* I had never be *gét*! (*had never
    been begotten*)

To my *sóul* a *fúll* | *gréat* | *próf*it it had *bé*, (*been*)

For *nów* I fear *páins* | *húge* and *gréat*.

The *tíme* | *pás*seth; || *Lórd* | *hélp*, that *áll* |
    wrought!

The *dáy* | *pás*seth | and is *ál*most agó; (*almost
    gone*)

I *wót* not *wéll* | *whát* for to *dó*!

The number of stresses, the length of line, the incidence of rhyme and alliteration seem almost fortuitous, and yet the passage has a shape, a sound-shape; it seems to balance itself. Here is a longer passage, taken from the climax of the play when *Everyman*, in true penitence for his sins, throws himself on the mercy of God; it should be spoken as it is felt, and I will therefore not disfigure it with italics and other typographical devices.

O eternal God, O heavenly figure,
O way of rightwiseness, O goodly vision,
Which descended down in a virgin pure,
Because he would Everyman redeem,
Which Adam forfeited by his disobedience;
O blessed Godhead, elect and high-divine,
Forgive my grievous offence!
Here I cry thee mercy in this presence.
O ghostly treasure, O ransomer and redeemer
Of all the world, hope and conductor,
Mirror of joy and founder of mercy,
Which illumineth heaven and earth thereby,
Hear my clamorous complaint, though it late be,
Receive my prayers! Unworthy in this heavy life
Though I be, a sinner most abominable,
Yet let my name be written in Moses' table!
O Mary, pray to the maker of all thing
Me for to help at my ending,
And save me from the power of my enemy,
For death assaileth me strongly. . . .

Let us take passages from *Murder in the Cathedral* for comparison: a principal difference is that Eliot often allows himself lines of far greater length, and carrying far more stresses than any in *Everyman*; for instance such lines as

And the *saínts* and *mártyrs waít*, for *thóse* who shall be

   mártyrs and *saínts*   (6)

Déstiny waíts in the *hánd* of *Gód*, | *sháping* the *stìll*

   un*sháp*en   (7)

148

Who *do* / some *well*, some *ill*, / *plan*ning and *guess*-
ing   (5)

*Hav*ing their *aims* / which *turn* in their *hands* / in the
*pat*tern of *time*.   (6.)

Here there are no rhymes, and almost no alliterations: but
there are repetitions of sound instead (saints and martyrs /
martyrs and saints / shaping / unshapen). A more *Everyman*-like passage might be

Your *thoughts* have *more* *pow*er than *kings* to com*pel*
you.   (4)

You have *al*so *thought*, / *some*times / at your *pray*ers,   (4)

*Some*times *hes*itating at the *an*gles of *stairs*,   (4)

And between *sleep* and *wak*ing, / *ear*ly in the *morn*-
ing,   (4)
When the *bird cries*, / have *thought* of *fur*ther *scorn*ing.   (5)

That *noth*ing *lasts*, but the *wheel turns*,   (4)

The *nest* is *ri*fled, and the *bird mourns*;   (4)

That the *shrine* shall be *pil*laged and the *gold* / *spent*   (4)

The *jew*els *gone* for *light la*dies' *orn*ament   (5)

The *sanc*tuary *brok*en, // and its *stores*   (3)

Swept into the *laps* of *par*asites and *whores*   (4).

Here we have alliteration in *pow*er-com*pel* and *light lad*ies,
but, as in *Everyman*, it is not so insistent as are the rhymes.
The total effect is one of living movement and emphatic
speech, that tumbles as if by accident on to the happy
rhythmical phrase and compulsive rhyme, unforeseeably,

and yet with gratification of a certain indefinable expectancy. These effects of verse are greatly enhanced by the intercalation of the two great prose scenes of the Sermon and the Knights' Apology, which provide their reasoned contrasts to the rest of the dialogue, where feeling predominates.

It may be helpful to offer an illustration of nineteenth-century blank verse, taken from a poetic drama of some repute, Tennyson's *Becket*. Few poets have had greater skill in this medium than Tennyson and I have chosen a speech that I hope will be thought fair to it:

Becket: Am I the man? That rang
Within my head last night, and when I slept
Methought I stood in Canterbury Minster
And spake to the Lord God and said 'O Lord,
I have been a lover of wines and delicate meats,
And secular splendours, and a favourer
Of players, and a courtier, and a feeder
Of dogs and hawks, and apes, and lions, and lynxes.
Am *I* the man?' And the Lord answered me,
'Thou art the man, and all the more the man.'
And then I asked again, 'O Lord my God,
Henry the King hath been my friend, my brother,
And mine uplifter in this world, and chosen me
For this thy great archbishoprick, believing
That I should go against the Church with him,
And I shall go against him with the Church,
And I have said no word of this to him:
Am *I* the man?' And the Lord answer'd me,
'Thou art the man, and all the more the man.'
And thereupon, methought, He drew toward me,
And smote me down upon the Minster floor.
I fell.

III

TENNYSON'S *BECKET*

It has become easy to disparage Tennyson and to do so is no part of my present purpose. The author of *In Memoriam* and *A Vision of Sin* will outstay his critics: he was less a dramatist than a poet, however, and his poetry suffers in his dramas. In this note I shall try to suggest why *Becket* fails where *Murder in the Cathedral* succeeds. I think the reasons lie a good deal deeper than those I have discussed in my note on the metre of *Everyman*. In the last resort the failure or success of a verse-play is not determined by the particular form of verse it happens to employ; versifica-tion is simply a kind of skill for organising the rhythms of language in one way rather than another; when an estab-lished way ceases, for the moment, to grip its hearers, a new one has to be found. When Christopher Marlowe was a young man, the rough and tumble versification of *Every-man* and of other Moralities and Interludes seemed to him to have lost its grip, and he introduced the newly-invented blank verse to the stage (following the stately example of *Gorboduc*, a play whose authors lacked his fiery skill) with all the swagger of an *avant-gardist* uttering a manifesto; he promised to deliver his hearers

> From jigging veins of rhyming motherwit
> And such conceits as clownage keeps in pay,

and offer them the 'high astounding terms' of blank verse in their place. And so he did. Eliot's manifesto is Marlowe's in reverse. He aimed to deliver us from the tedium of nineteenth-century blank verse; and so he did. But that is not the full explanation why Tennyson's Becket, compared with Eliot's, seems an impostor, and his play a failure, at least in twentieth-century eyes. Perhaps if we had seen and heard Irving in the part, as the nineteenth century heard him, we should have been deceived too. For originally the play was a thrilling success.

Now that all the glamour has melted from it, we can see where Tennyson went wrong: he was following a bad tradition. He was trying to *imitate* Shakespeare, as Wordsworth, Blake, Shelley, Keats, Beddoes, Byron and many others had tried before him. A tradition of imitation, of mere copying, can never produce anything but imitations and copies; it is like a factory that produces fake furniture. It imitates appearances and misses realities. It may achieve a reproduction but never a new creation. As Tennyson and Eliot both hit on the same subject, it is easy and interesting to compare their ways of setting about it.

Tennyson's *Becket* is in many ways the most successful piece of sham-Shakespeare ever written: he seeks to follow his master almost exactly. What he saw in his models was a chronicle structure, reinforced by a sub-plot. The former was based on historical fact (like Shakespeare's *Histories*) and the latter on a romantic love-story (like that in *The Winter's Tale*). He also saw that Shakespeare tended to include all classes of society in his plays, from king to beggar, so he imitated that; he observed that, generally speaking, the lower orders spoke a kind of comic prose and the more serious characters of higher rank spoke in blank verse. Professional Jesters spoke a tricky kind of prose, in an idiom of their own. The play-structure was a Five Act affair, and each Act had a number of scenes, usually scattered in an apparently haphazard succession of places, so as to alternate the various groups of characters and keep the sub-plot abreast of the main plot. Each scene had a little climax of its own, worked into the main narrative line, and in the last scene the story was completed and the conflict resolved, often in death.

All these formal characteristics Tennyson saw and imitated. He took the story of Thomas Becket from precisely the same sources as Eliot took them later, and followed them even more closely. That gave him his main plot. Then, following the lure of a sub-plot, he looked about for another source of interest. This was the first Will o' the Wisp to lead him astray. He found it in a late tradition or legend about Rosamond de Clifford ('the Fair Rosamond') which told how she had been the mistress of Henry II, kept by him in a secret bower at Woodstock; there she was discovered by Queen Eleanor (Henry's wife) and offered the alternatives of poison or dagger, and it is said she chose the former. She is believed to have been buried at Godstow Nunnery. To Tennyson, who had a special feeling for girls and gardens, and a hankering for melodrama, this legend was irresistible. There was only one difficulty: it was adulterous.

This, however, was not insuperable; at least he found a way round. First he was careful to leave it a mystery whether Rosamond had actually been married to Henry or not, while making it quite clear that it was a world-without-end love-match between them, that had brought them a little son, Geoffrey (children are useful for creating stage sentiment, as can be seen from the children in Shakespeare). Perhaps they had been secretly married long before, after all; and then political circumstances had forced Henry to marry Queen Eleanor. Be that as you may please to imagine, Queen Eleanor is represented as a villainess (something like the Queen in *Cymbeline*) and there is no suggestion of love between her and Henry. At the same time, it is strongly suggested (though not actually stated) that the love between him and Rosamond, though stronger than ever, is now a chaste, unconsummated love, in view of his being an officially married man, and that it only expresses itself in an occasional kiss bestowed on the Fair Rosamond's hand, received by her with quiet ecstasy:

> The happy boldness of this hand hath won it
> Love's alms, thy kiss (*looking at her hand*) Sacred!
>   I'll kiss it too. (*Kissing it*).

The total falsity of this situation is mortal to our interest in it; but worse is to follow. In order to gear it in with the main plot, Tennyson hit on the idea of making Henry ask Becket (in the early days of their friendship) to look after Rosamond for him while he was away in France, and tell him the secret way to her Bower. This, in effect, makes the Archbishop of Canterbury Warden of the King's Mistress, however idealistic their relationship may be. Into this preposterous idyll Queen Eleanor makes her way with cup and dagger and presents Rosamond with these terrible alternatives, unless she will instantly consent to marry Reginald Fitz Urse (another tie-up with the main-plot) who, it seems, has previously attempted to rape her ('He sued my hand. I shook at him. He found me once alone. Nay, nay, I cannot tell you!'). Luckily (though inexplicably) at the very moment when it seems Rosamond must choose between cup, dagger and Fitz Urse, Becket appears and the villain and villainess are foiled. Thus, led on by an attempt to imitate a Shakespearean sub-plot, Tennyson plunged into a melodrama, not only sickly in itself, but one which put his hero into a very false position. He attempted to retrieve it by making Becket convey Fair Rosamond (disguised as a monk) to a place of pious safety in Godstow Nunnery, and there she would have stayed, had she not been needed for the last Act. A rumour reaches

her there that Becket is about to excommunicate her
Henry, and she makes her way (still in her disguise) to
Canterbury, in an attempt to save him. She reaches it just
in time to be present at Becket's murder. The last stage
direction, as the curtain falls, is:

> De Brito, De Tracy, Fitz Urse *rush out crying 'King's
> men!'* De Morville *follows slowly. Flashes of lightning
> thro' the Cathedral.* Rosamond *seen kneeling by the body
> of Becket.*

The imitation of Shakespeare has led Tennyson further
from Shakespeare than if he had striven to avoid him.
Even the metre of *Everyman* could not have saved him.

This, however, was not all. Another Will o' the Wisp led
him into insincerities even worse. It was the lure of 'period'.
Tennyson lived in an age conscious of 'period' in a way
almost unknown to Shakespeare. This consciousness was
reflected in an attempt to secure accuracy in period costume on the stage; and it spread to the language. The play
is peppered with '*thee*' and '*thou*', '*yea*', and '*nay*' and a
hundred antique, or pseudo-antique, locutions, intended
to give it a mediaeval authenticity. King Henry swears '*By
God's eyes!*', and we feel dangerously close to the pure
Wardour Street of '*Odds Bodikins!*' and '*By my halidom!*'.
The language Shakespeare wrote was Elizabethan English.
To follow his tradition (as opposed to imitating him)
Tennyson ought to have written in Victorian English, as
Eliot wrote in Georgian.

It should be clear, even from this brief account of
Tennyson's *Becket*, and I think it clearer still when the
play is read in full, that the play has no *theme*. It is just a
piece of falsified history, told for the sake of its intrigue,
sentimentality, violence and spectacular effects. But it is
about nothing. Shakespeare's plays have their violences,

but they are centred in ideas. When he took hold of a story to dramatise, he looked into the causes in men and in history, and showed us patterns in their actions and in their sufferings: and that is why we derive an experience of meaning from them, a feeling that something wise and philosophical, that is disturbing and creative, is happening to us, as well as something exciting and poetical, while we watch. In his history plays, for instance, we see the spiritual form of England emerge in the struggle for power over her; it lives through all the alliances and cleavages, treacheries, devotion and carnage; we see a balanced consideration of the good and evil in men and women and of the ambiguities of their motives, and can recognise our own society and selves in theirs; we see problems in the nature of rulership, and above all the pattern of an historical process working itself out; it began with the crime of Richard II in murdering his uncle Gloucester, which brought on the greater crime of Bolingbroke's usurpation and the terrible retributions of civil war, enough to 'memorise another Golgotha'. And out of the long nightmare of the Wars of the Roses we are at last shown Henry Richmond, the first Tudor King, uniting the houses of York and Lancaster, and founding the golden age in which Shakespeare seems to have thought of himself as living, if we may trust what he says of it in his last play, *Henry VIII*, written ten years after the death of that extraordinary Queen and genius who was his patron. For in that play, at its last climax which shows us the infant Elizabeth, newly christened, in the arms of Archbishop Cranmer, he makes him say of her:

> In her days every man shall eat in safety
> Under his own vine, what he plants, and sing
> The merry songs of peace to all his neighbours.

God shall be truly known and those about her
From her shall read the perfect ways of honour,
And by them claim their greatness, not by blood.

He gives a moral shape to his vision of history that includes
his contemporary world in a panoramic significance; and
that is what most unifies these plays; he leaves us with
something to think about. And so does *Murder in the
Cathedral*.